CW00435119

'It is criminal that such a significant and brave action by Scottish soldiers is not afforded its rightful place. For that reason alone 4.5 Years *is worth reading... an honest and realistic account of Dave's experiences as he relives them through the pages of his book.'*
Scottish Association of the Teachers of History

'A fascinating Prisoner of War-Internee-Prisoner of War story. Dave's personality, technical skills, common sense and Scottish entrepreneurial attitude shine through. Interesting asides, explanations and information allow the young modern reader to understand the attitudes, the tensions, the subtleties and the realities of the time.'
Don Marshall, Military History Enthusiast

4.5 Years

David Taylor

© 2017 Jean Gill
The 13th Sign
All rights reserved.
ISBN 9791096459063
Cover design by Jessica Bell & Amie McCracken

Jean Gill's previous publications
Novels
The Troubadours Quartet
Book 4 Song Hereafter *(The 13th Sign)* 2017
Book 3 Plaint for Provence *(The 13th Sign)* 2015
Book 2 Bladesong *(The* 13th *Sign)* 2015
Book 1 Song at Dawn *(The 13th Sign)* 2015

Someone to Look Up To: a dog's search for love and understanding *(The 13th Sign)* 2016

Love Heals
Book 2 More Than One Kind *(The 13th Sign)* 2016
Book 1 No Bed of Roses *(The 13th Sign)* 2016

Looking for Normal (teen fiction/fact)
Book 2 Fortune Kookie *(The 13th Sign)* 2017
Book 1 Left Out *(The 13th Sign)* 2017

Non-fiction/Memoir/Travel
How Blue is my Valley *(The 13th Sign)* 2016
A Small Cheese in Provence *(The 13th Sign)* 2016
Faithful through Hard Times *(The 13th Sign)* 2017

Short Stories and Poetry
One Sixth of a Gill *(The 13th Sign)* 2014
From Bed-time On *(National Poetry Foundation)* 1996
With Double Blade *(National Poetry Foundation)* 1988

MAP OF WW2 FRANCE

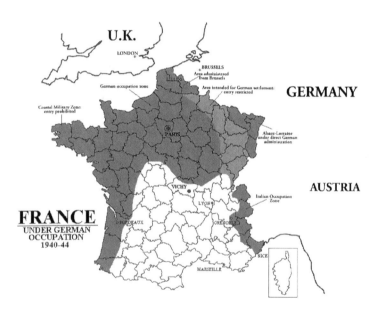

MAP OF DAVE'S JOURNEY
DURING 4.5 WAR YEARS

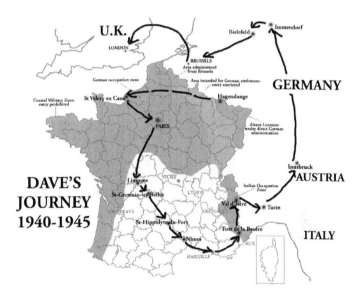

*For my children
and their children*

TABLE OF CONTENTS

FOREWORD

When I wrote to my Uncle Dave, I knew he lived in Canada and that he would be in his eighties, if he was still alive. I hadn't seen him or been in touch since we kept my father company for his last days in York Hospital, over ten years earlier

I was seeking information about his brother George, my father, so I could write *Faithful Through Hard Times*, based on my father's uncensored and illegal war diary. When an email popped up in my inbox from an email address that began 'Largo', I had an inkling that something important had happened. Largo was a beautiful fishing village on the east coast of Scotland, where Dave and George spent their childhood. Their Scottish roots remained important to them even though war left both of them changed beyond staying 'home'. Dave emigrated to Canada and George continued with the nomadic life of a soldier.

'We shall communicate like this from now on,' Dave wrote in his email, and so began a precious friendship. There was always a little rivalry between the brothers and at some point, he asked, 'Aren't you interested in *my* story?' and from then on, I spent my time on two Second World War fronts: researching and receiving news from my father in Malta, and also from my uncle, a Prisoner of War (POW) in France and Germany.

If you have listened to victims of trauma tell their story for the first time, as I have with students in my schools, you will know that the first time they speak out, there is an emotion, a catharsis, that is never repeated. Police and social workers have told me it is a pity the judges do not hear that first telling. If they did, there would be none of the questioning and cross-questioning as to whether it is the truth.

That is how it was for Dave. He was bitter at having lost 4.5 years of his young life. He chose the title and I think he would have added the number of seconds too. It mattered so much to him and underneath his energetic optimism, it mattered too that 'somebody' would read his account and understand what it was like. When you read this book, you are reading a witness statement.

A memoir like this is not a literary work and I deliberately kept it in Dave's own words, so you can hear his voice and listen to his memories. You have to read between the lines, know what he is remembering when he gives a spare tale of hardship and horrors. You have to know, as he did after the war, of the gas chambers and the Holocaust, to understand all that he implies.

Most of us know that Jews (if identified) were segregated from non-Jews but Dave also refers to the distinction between a POW and an Internee, between

Royal Air Force and ground soldiers, between nationalities, between officers and Other Ranks, all of which could make life more dangerous or just more uncomfortable.

Dave was sometimes considered to be an Internee, sometimes a POW. During the First and Second World Wars both sides set up internment camps to hold enemy aliens – civilians who were believed to be a potential threat and have sympathy with the enemy's war objectives. Internees were treated differently to prisoners of war and were usually given more privileges.

In theory, AXIS (Germany and its allies) subscribed to *The Geneva Convention,* an agreement as to how POWs should be treated. In practice, conditions varied, and starvation was common. Also, a soldier could be considered a spy for being 'disguised' in civilian clothing, or for wearing an enemy uniform instead of their own, and spies could be shot without justification.

In describing a soldier's 'duty to escape' and the 'systems' (i.e. escape routes), Dave notes in a matter-of-fact way that RAF officers were given priority because their training made them more valuable. It takes a few seconds before the reader realises that Dave is describing himself as more expendable, meaning that nobody cared about him and he was more likely to rot in jail, or even die, than were the pilots. These distinctions are not just rungs on a career ladder.

Political and national boundaries change daily in a war but what is important in understanding Dave's 4.5 years is to realise that at the beginning of his memoir, France was divided into northern occupied (by the Germans) and southern unoccupied territory. As the memoir makes clear, the south of France was not 'libre' (free) in reality but a German ally, increasingly governed by German diktats. Nowhere in France was safe for a British soldier and nobody could be trusted, whether in a camp or on the run, for reasons that Dave makes clear.

When I read Davina Blake's superb novel, 'Past Encounters', I was struck by the way she'd used POWs' true stories to construct a literary novel, giving detail to all that men went through in Dave's situation but would never express in such a way. If you read the two chapters she has kindly permitted me to include in this book, you'll understand all that Dave implies but does not say; the importance of having a 'mucker'(mate), the bond of shameful deeds, and the reception back home that, 'You had it easy.' I highly recommend 'Past Encounters' as a novel that sheds light on the experience of both the POW and the girl left behind, showing both the damage of war trauma and the hope of healing.

Dave's story and George's story shed light on each other and also on their parents in Scotland, waiting for news. Dave says that maybe I can imagine how his mother felt when he thoughtlessly sent a pair of new boots to his home address to keep them safe. Oh yes, I can imagine worrying every day about my two boys missing in action, and then receiving a pair of boots through the post, with no message. Neither wonder she too was changed by the war!

I hope you will read this little book slowly, aware of the amazing history behind each understatement, in respect for men like Dave and all they went through. Sometimes, he seems to be enjoying himself, putting all those inventive skills to solving problems, but he told me there was not one day went by that he didn't think about escaping.

Our emails, and, later, daily skype calls, covered family gossip, world events and all my news. Dave's excitement when he saw the first edition of his book was a joy to me. He had no idea what I was planning. We were with him in Toronto when it came through the post as a surprise gift and he had no tears as we left because he wanted to curl up and read his story right through.

He became an engineer after the war and had one patent to his name, a sewing-machine part. He told me that the time learning tailoring from his Jewish friend in the camp was time well spent. Dave loved to learn and he loved to teach; his Headmaster father would have approved. Without him, I would never have understood the mechanics of a 12th century papermill, necessary for my novel 'Song at Dawn'. I drew diagrams while he explained cams and water pressure over a skype line. He taught me how to coil a rope and how to use a kitchen table to ease backache (I was never convinced by that technique).

He always loved France, despite his time as a POW and when we moved from Wales to Provence, he wanted to know every detail of our adventures. His dry sense of humour could even catch me out sometimes, as when he wrote,

You know I don't think it such a good idea that you and John go to live in France, for John maybe, but I think the wine is the big attraction for you and I know a lot of (famous) writers were alcoholics, but being an alcoholic does not make you a better writer and you don't need it. Too bad you can't see the smile on my face. I know there are little symbols for emails to tell whether you're kidding or not but I don't know them and am too lazy to look them up. Well, I want to get this away and get on with my (almost last) episode. So once again you have brightened my life.

Love,
Dave

As he did mine, with his vivacity and his enthusiasm. I hope you too enjoy meeting Dave and hearing his story, starting with the first episode, signing up.

Editor, Jean Gill
1st November 2017
Dieulefit, France

1.

Before the war

In our house there was a photo of Dad in his Black
Watch uniform, complete with kilt and sporran. At
the beginning of the First World War, he joined
the Black Watch as a private soldier and did his basic
training in Catterick but, before he could be sent to
France, they recalled all teachers because they were
needed at home.

There was a special deal for teachers to go back to
university when they were demobbed (returned to
civilian life) and another special deal which said that
teachers could take a thing called Article 39, which
would be recognised as equivalent to a Bachelor of
Science degree, so Dad took this. He was a
Headmaster by the time it was our turn, my brother's
and mine, to go into uniform.

Dad could not afford university for both my
brother George and me at the same time, so I'd been
working in the tool design office of the National Steel
Foundry for a few years, while George went to
Dundee University, when it became understood by
everyone that a war was coming.

My Dad found me at around ten o'clock one night

and told me that unless I joined the Territorial Army by midnight I would be conscripted, and he asked what I wanted to do. I said I didn't mind if I was conscripted but I wondered whether I was in a reserved occupation.

We chased up to my boss's house only to find that he and his family were in bed asleep, so it was left at that, but then, about a week later, my Uncle Willie, who had connections with the local Territorial Branch of the Royal Signals, told my mother that he could get me into this branch rather than taking a chance of being conscripted into an Infantry mob, and that is the way I joined the Signals.

George, who was two years older, would not have been conscripted at this time, but he decided to join up. I was under the impression that university was not for him. Naturally, with his background in Chemistry, he preferred the Medical Corps and he showed up home one week-end to announce that he'd joined up for seven years.

I said, 'Are you out of your mind?!' Everybody else was joining up for the duration.

His answer was, 'It's going to last that long anyway.'

As it turned out, he was right on the money.

David Taylor's father (also named David Taylor)

2.

Home on leave for New Year, Jan,1940

George and I both got home for the New Year of 1940, on a week's leave, so Christmas had already passed, mine being spent in Badajos barracks, Aldershot, and I would guess that George spent his where I went to visit him once, in Crookham. The men there were in what were known as 'spiders', although I seem to remember they only had four legs, coming from a central hall.

I doubt if I saw him for more than a few minutes at home; he had his girl, Nettie, and I had mine, Gladys, so that accounted for most of the week. I think we only went home to sleep and get breakfast.

I can't remember any discussions with either of my parents other than army stuff. I already knew that this would be embarkation leave, and we left for France very shortly after that.

Because I could ride a motor cycle and the officer who was allocated one could not ride, I was given the bike to ride to Southampton and still had that bike up till we left the Maginot Line. After that, I was doing the job I was supposed to be doing, 2nd operator on a wireless truck.

3.

Travelling through France

Went to France, Le Havre, very cold winter, no water, pipes frozen.

We were actually read the riot act outside in the middle of the night for behaving badly when the officer and Sergeant Major came into the warehouse to find out why we were not starting our vehicles every two hours. Somebody reached up from the top bunk and jerked out the wiring for the lights, and then every epithet you ever heard and a few extra were shouted in the dark. Of course, they could not identify anyone, so we were told to get outside and that was it.

The only words I can remember are, 'You can be shot.'

We moved around a bit. The names I remember are Lillers, Bolbec, and then Steinwerk on the Belgian frontier. By that time, we were split into our signal section, 'K' Section, and attached to our Brigade, 153 of the 51st Highland Division.

Around February or March, we proceeded as a full convoy down to Hagondange, a steel making town in Alsace Lorraine, which was in the Saar, and which was behind the Maginot Line, that row of French fortified defenses built in the 1930s.

After a week or so there, we moved up to the Maginot and into the area of international outposts, and did whatever we were supposed to do, including learning by the sound where the shells were going. We were in the area known as the Black Forest, and German Patrols would infiltrate our positions at night, led by dogs that were trained to avoid human contact.

Then the German army broke through on the Belgian frontier, so we had to high-tail it up to Abbeville where we were doing well and even pushed the Germans back out of Abbeville. Unfortunately, the French retreated on our left flank, and we had to back up and head for Le Havre – Dunkirk was all over by this time.

As a radio operator who could also do shorthand, I used to write out the news from the BBC and post it outside the truck. This is what I wrote.

'It is now official that the last of the British Expeditionary has left France'.

About two days later, I wrote, *'It is now known that a famous highland fighting regiment is still fighting in the Abbeville area'.*

As we withdrew to try to reach Le Havre we were cut off by Rommel's tanks around Saint-Valery-en-Caux and that is when I was captured.

4.

Scarpering with Ken

We marched and marched and marched for three days and I'd had enough. None of the Kirkcaldy bunch would 'scarper' with me as they all wanted to get somewhere where we would be allowed to send a message home. I didn't see it like that and finally got one of our section to agree to go, Ken Coffin, a Dorset lad who had been conscripted and posted to the Signals as our mechanic. The march was terrible, nothing to eat, which I could handle, but thirst was the worst thing.

Anyhow, we took off (a story in itself) and got into a forest nearby where we met up with three French soldiers also on the loose, and we set up a camp hidden in the woods.

There were all sorts of equipment nearby, from an abandoned French artillery unit. Ken's father owned a garage in Dorset and Ken knew cars, trucks and motor cycles. We got two motor cycles going and petrol from an abandoned tank and were able to get around the area in search of food. No problem.

I took Merlin, one of the French guys, on the back of the bike to a field where there were cows, which he knew how to milk, and there were lots of wild strawberries around. This was a daily occurrence and naturally we had strawberries and cream whenever we wanted.

We got to know a youth from the village and he would bring us food, and that's where I learned to kill and pluck a goose. There was also quite a bit of dry goods beside the artillery unit stores – rice, potatoes and a barrel of French issue wine.

The time frame for this would be: captured, I think June 12th 1940, three days later escaped, lived in the woods about a week then were warned by the kid that the Germans were coming to salvage the French equipment, and we moved all the gear that we'd collected, to another forest not very far away. Two trips on the bikes to move everything, including tents etc.

By this time, the young guy had spoken to two daughters of the farm in the village, and he brought them to our camp, complete with baked goods for us poor guys, and a duck.

Merlin was the typical country boy who knew how to cook anything, so he and I were good friends because I was also brought up in the country and we made a good team.

The two girls invited Pierre, another of the French guys, to come to the farm. When he returned, he said we were all going to live at the farm. Pierre went back and the next day the farmer came to our camp with a horse and wagon, loaded all our stuff and covered it up and we rode the wagon back to the farm.

It so happens that there was a Yugoslavian woman driving a yellow Salmson sports car, who was bringing dry goods from Paris to the farm and taking back butter and eggs and chickens, (early black market). She carried a message to Pierre's wife in Paris, who showed up with her father at the farm.

After a day or two, Pierre, his wife and his father-in-law took off for Paris along with Bobbie, the third member of our group. Somehow or other, by searching some of the bodies that were still lying around, they had papers that stated that they were unfit medically or what is known as *'prestataires'*.

That left Ken and me around the farm to eat some marvellous meals, and drink cognac in the evening, some of the other villagers bringing goodies for the poor Anglais.

Then the Yugoslavian lady showed up again, Madam Cheret, whose husband was Fred Cheret, a well-known jockey. It was decided that we were all going to Paris in her car, except that we were going to make it appear that she'd picked us up, so we left the farm on bicycles that Ken and I fixed up, and headed on our way.

Along came Madam Cheret and we tied the bicycles on the back of the car and squeezed in. We didn't get very far when we were stopped by a German patrol. Madam Cheret stopped as fast as she could, a good way behind the patrol car, got out and walked to meet the German officer.

She produced the papers she carried, signed by a high-ranking officer, saying that as a Yugoslavian she could go wherever she wanted and had a petrol allowance to do it. He read the paper, stepped back and saluted. Madam Cheret walked back to the car and we drove on, reaching Paris that same evening and going to Bobbie's parents' home. They moved us into a flat for the night, and the next day Madam

Cheret took us to her home.

A few days later, she found out where her husband was, and had to go and see him and take some food and clothes, so she moved us to a friend's house. The friend was shacking up with an American, who was driving an ambulance for the American hospital.

During this time we visited the British Legion Headquarters and scared them out of their wits. They expected German soldiers to walk in right behind us.

We were in civvies since the farm, which meant that we no longer had the Geneva Convention rights of soldiers. If the Germans caught us, we could have been charged with spying and shot.

We then crossed the road to the American Embassy and the only help we got was advice to get to a seaport, hit a sailor over the head and steal his papers (assholes).

Two years older, I might have done that.

Then we had to move again and went to live with Bobbie's sister, Madame Bordes, who worked in an '*imprimerie*', a print-shop, right opposite Notre Dame. Ken and I went in the metro to the *imprimerie* where she worked, given instructions from Bobbie who didn't want his parents to know. She then took us to her apartment and we lived there for a week or more.

We did some wiring jobs around the house, and that is the first time I ate horse meat from the butcher; it is very good when it is from a horse reared for meat. Sunday was a day off work, and she showed us around the west bank where the artists are, and up through Montmartre to the Eglise du Sacré Coeur. So we were standing there, with German officers all around taking pictures – remember that Paris was an open city.

Being able to read and speak French, I was able to read the posters going up all over that stated that anybody caught harbouring British soldiers could be shot, so I told Ken that we had to get out of there, and Bobbie's sister agreed.

By this time, we knew there was an unoccupied France and also that there was a zone *'non-occupé'* (unoccupied) in the Pas de Calais, then a zone *'interdit'* (unauthorized) north of that on the Channel, so we decided to go south.

Bobbie's sister's husband was in the navy and was in unoccupied France trying to get north, and we were in Paris trying to get south. With some food from the sister, and a few instructions, we took the metro as far as we could go south, then walked and walked and walked. This would be the middle of July, I would estimate.

5.

Heading south

We, Ken and I, headed due south out of Paris past Orly Airport, and on and on. We said we would do thirty kilometres every day. This was in daylight, and the first night we broke into an empty house, as a lot of them were at that point. We found some food but, most importantly, there was a calendar, issued by an insurance company, on a wall, with a small map of France as the picture, about ten inches square, and on this calendar was shown the river Cher, and also a railway line that fizzled out just north of the river. That was where we were heading and we walked on in daylight for the next three or four days, thirty kilometres each day, usually finding someplace to sleep but keeping away from villages and towns.

About this time, we decided to change to walking at night and ultimately found our railway, which seemed to be disused, so we walked on that for two or three nights. We got to the end of the line where we slept in a haystack for a little while, then walked south again, a hundred yards or so through a farm in the early morning. There we came to a stream that looked fairly deep, so we backed up to the farm and knew somebody was watching us.

Then this man came out from an open door, and we told him what we were and where we wanted to go. He took us into the house and gave us breakfast. I still remember an old lady sitting there and saying over and over *'pauvre gosses'*, 'poor kids'. At that time I didn't really know the word but I knew what she meant.

After some talk, he asked us if we were ready to go. We said *oui* and off we went. He first went into a barn and came out with a long plank of wood over his shoulder, walked down to the stream where we'd already been, stood the plank on end and let it fall over the stream, then motioned for us to follow him across.

We then walked to another stream which was almost the same, where the action was repeated, then another and into a wood where he stopped pointed to a river and said, 'That is the Cher'.

Away to our left we could see German soldiers in their underwear doing early morning calisthenics. The farmer shook our hands, wished us luck and advised that we wait there till it got dark, then cross the river.

For reasons which I have not gone into, we'd learned that people could help you then protect themselves by 'shopping' you. Ken was actually the one who said, 'Let's cross now', and I thought it was the logical thing to do. Most of the distance to the river would be under cover of trees, and it was only a short distance.

We had already been told that it was not deep at that time of the year, so off we went and got down to the river bank and, without taking any clothes off, went across; me, where I could see ripples but Ken, without the experience I had from back home in Kennoway, tried to cross where it was flowing more narrow but much deeper and I had to go back and drag him out.

On the other bank, we had to scramble up to the top, never knowing when we might get a bullet in the back. I'm sure they must have seen us. On the other side, Ken, who could not speak any French, was desperate to find someone to ask if we were in unoccupied France. He had not followed any of the conversation I'd had with the farmer.

I knew we had made it, but he saw a man across the field ploughing, and would not be convinced until we asked him, so off we went up to the man and I asked him in my best French, '*Ici, c'est France non-occupé?*'

He said, '*Ici France, là bas, Allemagne*' – even Ken got that.

6.

In transit

After crossing the Cher and getting a few directions from the locals we reached a railway station somewhere and bought tickets for Limoges. We wanted to get to a big city before saying, 'Here we are, now what?'

As I said, we crossed the river early morning and we arrived in Limoges late evening. We found that there were lots of people wandering around like us and the authorities had opened a cinema where we could sleep. I don't recommend trying to sleep in a cinema between the seats and on a floor that slopes down.

Next morning we made ourselves presentable, and walked into the main Gendarmerie, told them who we were and how we got there. Obviously, I had to do most of the talking. They didn't believe our story, although we still carried our army paybooks, so they transferred us to the *'deuxième bureau'*, the second office, where we went over the whole thing again but they still seemed to think we were some kind of spies.

We were next taken to an army barracks and finally we got some food – the first decent meal in about seven days. As it was not a regular meal time, we were taken to the cookhouse, were introduced to the cooks and could get anything we wanted.

After we had eaten and were wondering what to do next, I pulled out my trusty chromatic harmonica, which I carried with me no matter what, and started playing a few tunes for the cookhouse staff. This was a great success and the next thing was that I was invited to play in the officers' mess that night. Things were really picking up.

The commanding officer said he would take us out the next day and buy us some clothes, but unfortunately the next day two gendarmes walked in and said they were taking us to a camp where there were some other British soldiers, and would we please put these handcuffs on as we were going by train and they didn't want us to escape.

I said in my best French, 'Don't be stupid, if this place is as good as you say it is, why would we want to escape? We can easily escape if we don't like it there, so please remove the handcuffs.' They did.

7.

St Germain les Belles

Where we arrived was in a camp with the title *'Centre de Séjour Surveillé'*, in a little village called St-Germain-Les-Belles, which you can find on the map. There were three other English soldiers there with stories much like ours, plus about a hundred Jewish men from France and Germany who were trying to get to the U.S.A.

After being assigned our sleeping quarters and meeting the other guys, we were given the 'griff' on what things were like, which included the fact that we were officially Internees, and were allowed freedom in this village – only us, not the Jews. We made our life here for the immediate future.

The main point of this episode is that the Jews I referred to were all men, mostly older types except one who had just got married recently in Holland to the daughter of the Burgomeister, and his wife was living in the village.

We British people were free to go anywhere in the immediate vicinity provided we returned at night and I managed to talk the camp commandant into letting Karl Rosenberg go out with us on parole. All the others were confined to the camp and spent most of their time on educating each other.

One gentleman whose name was Mendelssohn and who claimed to be related to the well-known one, wanted to write a piece of music for me to play on the harmonica, and when I said I couldn't read music, he wanted to teach me.

They had classes for English, as they were all waiting for visas to go to the U.S.A. (some hopes) and asked us to help. They had classes for everything. The weather was great then and they would sit on benches outside, and learn and learn. That's when I learned to admire the Jewish people.

There were no Jews in our barrack-room, but there were some other nationalities without proper papers. One was a Spanish radio engineer, and not knowing Spanish except for the swearwords, which he used frequently, we communicated by me writing one half of a mathematical equation and he would write the other half if something equalled something else, or we would write various formulas just to find out what each of us knew. Our usual greeting was to convey that we had another formula. It may not seem like fun to you but it was communicating.

When Ken and I got to the camp, the other U.K. soldiers had already written to the American consul in Clermont-Ferrand (the Spanish guy had worked in the radio station there) and they sent us application forms for U.K. people in distress and who needed money. These forms allowed us to draw ten pounds per week to be repaid later.

'Great,' we thought, and took the forms to the camp commandant and asked him if we could rent a house somewhere that we could live in – that was a lot of money then.

He came back a few days later and gave us the names of two towns we could live in and report to the Gendarmerie every week but this was not to be. The consulate advised us that they had been in touch with the British Government and we would be allowed a pound per week once they got it organised. Well, what were we to do for coffee money in the village? And by that time, we'd developed a taste for other things to drink.

Being free to wander around, and as this was early autumn, we found all kinds of fruit and nuts in the woods which we could eat to supplement our diet. In fact, there were more than we could eat, so we would bring some back to the camp.

Karl, our friend, was not allowed out with us yet and I brought a tin cup of raspberries back for him. That was the start. One of the Jews was at the gate as I came in and he offered to buy the raspberries. Although they were not at liberty, they seemed to have lots of money so we started going out every day to see what we could drum up; apples, pears, Spanish chestnuts, and anything else that showed up. This gave us enough money to go out at night and visit the bistros and cafes and make friends with the locals.

There were also some French soldiers in the village and one of them was a great jazz music piano player (he claimed to have played with the Quintet du Hot Club in Paris – he could have been telling the truth) and he could accompany me on my harmonica, which was always good for a drink or two.

There was another restaurant in the village, where I played almost every night. The Patron would always bring me a glass of his special cognac as I was good for business, but unfortunately this kept me busy and left Ken to try his hand with the daughter, which worked out OK for him.

Because of the climate, windows were wide open and every night the girl had to go for milk, so she would stand outside the window in the dark and rattle the milkcans, then Ken would nip out the window and a while later, back in again. And here was I still playing the harmonica – what an idiot.

My 'mucker' (partner) Ken was a full-time barber before being called up, working in his Dad's garage at night, so with the four others, Syd, Jake, another one we called Popeye and one other, we got together and bought a complete set of barber tools – razor, scissors, comb, and strop – on condition he would cut our hair, and give us the odd shave now and again.

Of course, he was free to go into business for himself with the wealthy Jews. This deal continued for me for a long time, but not for the other four after we left St. Germain. It was another source of income which Ken and I always shared and we were never without money in our pocket.

We must have been there about six weeks at least and, by that time, I'd arranged with some local farmers to supply me with eggs. We, Ken and I, had been selling a few dozen up to that time but I finally arranged for about ten times that amount and, just when everything was going so well, we were informed that we would be leaving. I don't know if we knew then that we were going to Marseille but that is where we landed.

8.

Fort St Jean

I realise that I could have said a lot more about the Jews and the possible outcome of their *'Séjour'*, their 'stay'. I have often thought about writing to the newspaper in *Letters to the Editor* to try to find out if any of them survived. Somebody here in Canada must know about St-Germain-Les-Belles. I am just too lazy. Most of the survivors, if any, would be dead by now anyway of natural causes.

I don't remember much about the trip to Marseille except for passing a large railway junction on the way, with rail lines crossing at right angles, something I had never seen before. We arrived in Marseille and proceeded to Fort Saint Jean, the Foreign Legion depot. It stood on the south side of Le Vieux Port with Fort Saint Mark on the opposite side. There was a transporter bridge just a little bit into the city.

We were then attached to the Foreign Legion as Detachment 'W', given a card which stated this fact and allocated a large room where we could sleep on wooden two tier bunk beds, on straw palliasses and a blanket.

Within an hour I was bitten to death – nobody had

told us about the bed bugs. You know soldiers had to go over their metal beds with blow lamps? This is not a one-time deal as the bugs are back in days. The worst thing is the smell when you kill them. You get very sensitive to anything moving beside your skin and we could kill them even in the dark. You knew by the smell that you had got one.

The French had got all the British guys together by this time and there were almost two hundred, about fifty per cent Scottish. We were free to come and go as we pleased, provided we returned each night. We soon got to know the city and walked all over, from the Cannebière to the east where we could see the Chateau d'If and north up the mountain.

Food rationing had been on for a while and we had no ration cards. Food was only what we got at the meals in the fort, and it was not enough, so we tried the Red Cross and got absolutely no help from them, also the Seamen's Mission where some British merchant seamen were living under the auspices of the Reverend Donald Caskie, who after the war wrote a book. They were getting food from somewhere but we could not get any of it. We had a very poor opinion of the Reverend.

Somehow, I don't remember how, I got the address of a Mrs Grace, an English woman living in Nice, so I wrote to her and we got corresponding. She asked what I needed, and I said, Money and clothes'. She asked me to send my measurements and a photograph if I had one, so I got my picture taken in the city and sent her both.

A short time later, she sent me a very nice new sports jacket and some money and asked if I needed books. Obviously, I said yes and she sent me a package of books. She'd already asked me if I liked mystery books and she sent me some Edgar Wallace. Two or three of the books she sent were signed by the author *'To my dear friend Mrs Grace.'*

One thing she said after she got my photograph was, 'You will never be out of work'. It seemed a strange thing to say at the time but she was proved right. More about Mrs Grace later.

We were still in Fort St. Jean at Christmas and I still have a copy of our Christmas Day menu designed by one of the guys, with an excellent sketch of the fort on the front, including a tiny little stick person jumping from the top into the water, which had actually been done for a bet. The top must have been about ninety feet above the water.

We left there in early New Year 1941 because we were causing too much trouble in Nice with the French sailors, whom we blamed for not coming to our side, and they blamed us for sinking a lot of their boats when they would not switch. So off we went to St-Hippolyte-du-Fort (check that one out).

Fort St Jean, Marseille, in 2010

9.

St Hyppolyte du Fort

St. Hippolyte, as you may know, was a military school – for cadets I think – and was where we were when we were first visited by the American consul and put on the payroll. I can't remember how much we got at that time but our army pay was only two shillings a day when we joined up, for a private soldier, and we must have got about that in the equivalent francs. At that point, we were free to go outside the fort any time.

We discovered that it was impossible to buy any food and the rationing was getting worse. Ken and I also discovered that we could go to the local hotel and buy a meal. The food was not too substantial but it helped out. Unfortunately, we could only do this every second day, our finances being what they were, even with the money we both had saved up. We were the only ones who knew about this so we were lucky.

We now had three officers (British) in command, who saw to the pay arrangements and not much else at that point. There were approximately two hundred British soldiers in the fort and we soon got a soccer team started. The French were able to supply boots, balls and strip and before long we were playing against the local team every Sunday and usually winning, to the point where we wanted to join the local league. This was eventually arranged and our first game away was in Arles so we all got on the train and off we went. Well, it was a disaster. The referee called a very bad game by British standards, which resulted in a break-in at the end of the game. Needless to say, that was the end of being in the league.

The next episode was that somebody decided to organize a whist drive in the recreation room where there were tables and benches. This finished up with accusations of cheating and a real brawl broke out with overturned tables and benches thrown all over. I am not sure if the riot erupted out of the room and into the rest of the building and finished up with a Scotland versus England battle in the rooms and passage-ways but that certainly happened, although they may have been separate items, the result being that they finally decided we could not be allowed out and locked the gate.

While we were still free, things were not too bad. There was a cinema which opened on Sunday afternoon and as Ken and I both had girl-friends at that time, we could take them to the cinema (English subtitles). My friend was French and Ken's was Spanish, the town being a place with a lot of refugees from the Spanish war. Ken did look a little Spanish, coming from Dorset – probably from the smuggling trade years back.

It was a pity the freedom ceased. Thinking back now, I realise that had we got back to the U.K. we would have gone right back into the army but that never entered our minds then. The only thing we thought about was getting out of there now that we were locked up.

The British officers were allowed out on parole, which didn't improve our attitude and, by that time, they had been joined by a few RAF escapees and they had control of our money. Originally we got this every month but due to the fact that there had been several attempts at escape, the French decided we could only get weekly payments, so that if we escaped we would not have much money to get anywhere.

Now, if you did want money to escape, the first thing you had to do was tell the officers how you intended to get out and they would send RAF people first because it took so much longer to train flyers. Luckily, Ken and I both had money of our own so when we decided it was time to go, we went.

We got out with a few little problems and walked to Nîmes where we got a train to Perpignan and stayed overnight, then got a bus which would take us to Arles (a different Arles) where we had an address to go to.

Unfortunately, before we got there, two gendarmes came on the bus and started asking for 'papers' so we presented them with our army paybooks. This was not what they were looking for, so they took us off the bus at the next town which had a gendarmerie. Then they took us into a restaurant, arranged that we got a good meal with the usual chopine de vin, then took us in for the usual questions and finally locked us in a cell. While on the bus, I stuck my cigarettes up one sleeve and a box of wooden matches up the other.

This worked fine when they searched us until they

said to me, *'Levez les bras,'* and the stupid matches rattled.

The officer said, 'He's got matches,' which they took but they didn't get the cigarettes.

They were nice enough to put us both in the same cell where we spent the next few hours rubbing things together to light a cigarette, unsuccessfully – two girl guides would have come in useful (to rub two sticks together or whatever). I think it was the next day at the one and only mealtime when we heard the keys rattle and, before they opened the door, I stuck a cigarette in my mouth and walked out to the courtyard where the soup was being dished up.

One of the guards was smoking, so I walked up to him, said, *'Tu as du feu?'* and stuck my cigarette in his face to get a light.

A few seconds later, he realised I was smoking and marched me in to see the Officer again.

I told him we were not criminals and asked if we could have our matches back. I must have put up a good argument because he allowed us to keep the cigarettes and matches.

Two days later, they came in to tell us about this great place where they were sending us, where there were lots of other British soldiers and we would be fed and life would be just grand. If they had questioned us, how did they not know we had just come from there?

A few months ago, some of our guys had been brought back to Marseille after succeeding in getting into Spain. They gave themselves up in Spain, and, expecting to be sent home via Portugal, they told the truth about where they had come from, got stuck in jail and got returned, ultimately, in poor shape, to

Marseille, as Internees, not as escaped Prisoners-Of-War. So we had told them that we'd escaped and travelled down via Bordeaux with no mention of being Internees. Inside the barracks at St Hippolyte we were considered Internees but if we escaped, and were caught, we were safer showing our army paycards and being treated as POWS. It was complicated.

We were then escorted back to where we'd come from, where we got fifteen days solitary confinement for first escape.

This is where Mrs Grace comes in again. She'd sent her entire library to St. Hippolyte and a library was set up in a room which the French gave us. During that fifteen days I was reading two books per day. We had two fifteen-minute exercise periods each day which gave me time to get to the library and get another book.

The walls of the cell were whitewashed and I managed to get hold of a pencil, so, when I was not reading, I was decorating the walls. The battle of the River Platte had taken place about that time, so with the names of all the boats etc I did a complete mural of the battle on one wall. I was always good at drawing battle-ships and cruisers.

On another wall it was mostly race cars and I finished up standing my bed on end so I could do the ceiling. After I'd finished my fifteen days, the guards would bring their wives and kids in to see the cell. As you will find out as the story continues, I never had a problem passing the time.

I am fairly sure this happened after we were locked in. On the radio, which we had that day tuned to the BBC, we heard that a well-known pilot had been shot down. They gave you his name as an American, Whitney Strait, who had volunteered to fly for Britain.

We all said at the same time, 'He will be here shortly,' and he was.

His wife was from a very well-known rich American family, I believe. He had no problem getting parole to move around St. Hippolyte but within a short time we realised what an asshole he was. Somewhere in the next month or two, he arranged that there would be a medical board and if you were reckoned unfit for future service by French military standards, you would be re-patriated. Well the board took place and W. S. was one of those who passed (or failed as planned, depending how you look at it). Then it was a matter of waiting till everything was organised, which took some time.

While all this was taking place, he got us all out on the parade ground and told us that while they were waiting to be re-patriated there would be no attempted escapes. It was well known in the army that a prisoner's duty is to try to escape, and to hear an officer tell you this caused everyone to say that the S.O.B. should be court-martialed.

During this period, two things took place: one was that I managed to get on a work party cutting grapes and taking them to the crushers at the back of the farmhouse. Being able to speak French, I talked a bit to the daughter of the owner of the vineyard and found out that they knew how to get people on the 'scheme' to get people out of the country.

The other thing was that my buddy Ken had got a job in the cookhouse and one of the other guys told Ken he'd found a way out, Ken had already told him that I had a connection outside so Ken was asked whether Dave would tell him where he should go. Well I did tell him and he escaped as planned.

The French knew he was gone on the roll call and W. S. started questioning people and finally got to Ken whom he threatened with all kinds of things until Ken told him where he'd gone, so W.S. went to the farm where the arrangements were being made, and brought the guy back. He claimed that he did this in order to not endanger the people at the vineyard. Well, he was crap from there on. Ultimately, the 'unfit' people get away.

A little aside to that story is: several RAF pilots landed up in St. Hippolyte and one of them had a beautiful pair of leather fur-lined flying boots which I bought for a package of tobacco. I talked one of the re-patriation people into wearing them back to Britain, then shipping them to my home.

This all took place as planned as I found out when I got home and there were the boots. I never gave any thought to how my mother would feel when the boots arrived parcel post. You can maybe imagine how she felt. I ultimately got a friend to sole and heel them, and, by that time, I had a motor cycle so the boots, together with a surplus flying suit, set me up for any weather.

Working in the vineyard is one of the more pleasant memories I have. You had a special little hooked knife for cutting the stems, and dropping the grapes into the container then, with another guy to help you, you got the container on your back and walked up to the house. The two girls walked around all day with trays of wine glasses, and we would eat grapes – only those taken from the side exposed to the sun. They were hot and just burst in your mouth. Every night I would take a sack of grapes back and dump them out on the floor and say, 'Help yourself,' after making sure Ken got his first.

Talking about grapes, there was a product which we could buy in the village when we were free. It was called *'sucre du raisin'* and came in large blocks. The shopkeeper would cut a chunk off and put it on a piece of brown paper. Fudge would be the nearest equivalent. It was the nearest thing to sweets we could get.

I think I said earlier that Whitney Strait was Chairman of BOAC after the war – BOAC didn't exist then – it was BAC. He was a member of the Whitney family, (like in Eli Whitney, inventor of the cotton gin), also of the Vanderbilt and the Strait families. By coincidence, I hired his maintenance mechanic, John Williams, as a tool designer here in Toronto. When we found this out, he brought in photos of W.S. and him standing beside his Spitfire. Of course, I didn't realise any of this when I hired him.

Now, to proceed with the Taffy Wright story, I must give you some background first. With over two hundred men in this 'school', various misdemeanors took place like petty theft, poor hygiene, (getting body lice and not looking after yourself) to the extent that we would strip somebody naked, scrub him and burn the clothing. So it was decided that we needed our own jail.

The French went along with this and Corporal Wright (ex Sergeant) was given the job of jailer. We usually had one or two in jail for one reason or another. There was also a room in the 'school' where the people who ran the camp lived (a Sergeant Major, two or three Non-Commissioned Officers, all the men who worked in the cookhouse, and Corporal Wright, including of course my buddy Ken).

Now we can get on with the story. One night, the men in this room began to realise that Taffy had been drinking a little more than his little cup of wine we got with each meal, so they watched him as he went out for a while and returned a little more inebriated, until they decided to follow him.

It was dark, of course, but they saw him go to the store room where the food and wine was kept and surprise, surprise, he opened the door and went in, coming out again a little later even more stewed but remembering to lock the door. Taffy, being an old regular soldier, had discovered that the keys to the room where our cells were, also opened the wine cellar door.

This all came out later, but at this time, after a few more trips, good old Taffy was too drunk to bother about locking the door and initially only the people in this one room were aware of a golden opportunity. Ken, being Ken, came up to the room where I was, bearing gifts of wine – you can't keep a secret like this forever and within the next couple of hours, people were looking for containers to put the wine in.

Now I must leave the story for a minute. When rations are extremely low and you are on the verge of starvation (this was the worst time for food in the 4.5 years) you can't sleep when you are extremely hungry plus you urinate much more frequently and urgently. The lavatories were outside in the courtyard (parade ground) and it got cold at night, so five litre cans that the so-called jam came in, were valued as something you could keep under the bed, and empty in the morning. I know you are ahead of me right here but that is what happened. The cans were washed out and filled with wine.

Sooner or later it had to happen – the French found out what was going on. With two hundred people all drunk on red wine it was pretty obvious, especially when they are all wandering around carrying their cans and singing army songs. So they herded us all back to our respective rooms and proceeded to carry out a bed-to-bed search to see who had wine. The French commandant, accompanied by several guards, did the checking. At least, the guards did the checking. If three or four guys were in a group of buddies, only one can was needed, so not all the cans contained wine.

The commandant demanded that the contents of each one be ascertained while we stood by our beds, standing up as well as we could – not easy when you are almost falling down laughing while the commandant is getting madder and madder. I don't remember any repercussions after this event. There must have been but my memory fails me.

Unlike my brother George, I would eat anything, including the octopus they served us in St. Hippolyte, even if it was full of sand. The only problem I had was when I was called up and was forced to drink tea for the first time. I would not drink anything but milk up to that point. I could not understand the rush to get a fire going to make tea whenever we stopped after a long convoy and I was starving. The rest didn't care when the food would be available as long as they got their tea. I don't think I ever got over that.

Sure, I drank tea but to me it was, and is still now, unimportant. (Says he, sitting typing this with a beer right beside him. I hardly ever drink beer all winter but in the hot weather there is nothing that will quench your thirst like a bottle of beer. The last three days have been gorgeous for golf, with clear blue skies and just enough breeze to keep it from getting too hot. 18 holes every day. Gladys says, 'Surely missing one day would not kill you.' I keep telling her it might but she doesn't believe me).

If you want nicknames, I was called 'Doughts', pronounced that way but probably not spelled that way, most Davies in our village were called by that nickname, from a little rhyme which was *'Davie douts, the laird of louts'*. All Welshmen were Taffies and that was from the children's rhyme *'Taffy was a Welshman, Taffy was a thief, Taffy came to our house and stole a lump of beef'*. If you don't know that, your education has been sadly neglected.

Other nicknames: Lofty, Tich, Geordie, Scouse, Haggis (more common than Jock in the Second World War), Brummie. My own nickname in the army was Tyke, mostly known as *the* Tyke; 'if you want anything or need anything, go see the Tyke'. I will probably think of a lot more in the next few days.

My original chat room name was Tyketalk, but people thought I was ten years old so I dropped it. I went to '90Jag' and they wanted to know if I was actually 90 and did I have a lot of money and would I like to get married? so I gave up on chat rooms. You can't win.

The other nicknames I remember were my partner in the radio truck in the army, Jimmy Redpath (his father was a dentist in Kirkcaldy) who was over six feet and was called 'Whangy' and another in Fort St. Jean who was called 'Depth Charge Rupert' for the same obvious reasons.

St. Hippolyte was the worst for starvation in all the 4.5 years because as Internees we were not eligible for Red Cross parcels. This covered about six months and then we received a shipment of bulk food from Argentina. There was steak, corned beef, sausages, all tinned of course, and dished out by the British Officers.

The first issue was one tin of bully beef each. Big mistake. Everybody got severe 'runs' because we'd not had any fat in our diet for months and we could not handle it, so it became one tin between two or three or four, depending on the contents. We soon got used to it and life improved greatly.

Somewhere during the bad period, I developed a skin problem shaving in cold water and went to hospital in Nîmes. The first thing they did was take my clothes away and stick me in a beautiful hot bath, then they forgot to come back and the water was cold so I was debating getting out in my birthday suit and going looking for some-one, then a nurse showed up with my back-to-front gown and I went for treatment.

They had a gadget that blew water vapour all over your face and I don't remember what then but it finished up with a total covering of gentian violet. In actual fact, I knew when I got out of the bath that it was already healing so it didn't take more than a few days to completely heal.

When the doctor examined my face during the treatment he said it was *'petit'* something. Later that day the penny dropped, *'im-petit-go'* not spelled like that but pronounced in French like that.

The whole reason for telling this story is that after treatment each day we could walk around the hospital, only locked in a cell at night, and I got talking to a French teacher who was in for something and who told me that he studied phonetics. He asked whether, if he wrote something in French, I would translate it into idiomatic English which he would then write using his phonetic system and repeat back to me. The system worked so well he finished up with a real Scottish accent. It was then that I realised what a strong accent I had.

10

Fort de la Revère

It must have been around August 1940 by this time, when escape over the Pyrenees would be still possible, that they decided to move us to an escape-proof place.

Now you can look up Fort de la Revère on the map. It is right on top of the mountain south-west of La Turbie, and was a naval defense fort from away back, complete with moat, drawbridge, catwalk all around which the sentries used to use, and the barrack-rooms were roofed over with earth and sod. One end of the room exited onto the catwalk and the other end into a passage that exited out to a parade ground in the middle of the fort.

We had only got to our rooms and grabbed beds when all the lights went out. Somebody shorted out the whole system, and as the French were new to this place and didn't know where anything was, they immediately locked all the doors as fast as they could get us herded into our rooms.

Next morning, on the coiled barbed wire (which completely filled the moat and was stretched from one side to the other) were just a few rags of clothing about half-way over and two guys were gone. So much for the escape-proofing.

From the top of the building where the earth and sod was, we could look down on: the Mediterranean, Cap Ferrat, the Grand Corniche, Eze, Villefranche, Monte Carlo, and, away to the left, Italy. One day we were up on top when we heard an aeroplane, and everybody looked up – the plane was actually away below our eye level.

We did get Red Cross parcels both from Canada and the U.K. in the Fort, and we also got British army uniforms and army boots. I was also able to buy a camera and had quite a few photos taken in the fort of myself, Ken and others in our group, and photos taken looking down from the top of the Fort. Then, one day, they decided we would all assemble on the parade ground in our uniforms and I had a picture of that, all nicely at attention by rooms.

I also had photos of a boxing night we organised. We built a ring on the parade ground and invited some guests. The Prince of Monaco, the American consul and aide, the Camp commandant, and some French Non-Commissioned Officers – I had pictures of them all. I still had these pictures up until a few years ago and then I lost them.

This was a great night and the star of the evening was Sergeant Gerry Nabarro, a Public School boy who volunteered to fight the guy who we recognised as our toughest boxer. Gerry knocked him out in the first round; they must have taught boxing at his school. His father was a Member of Parliament and he comes into the story again later. Flight Sergeant Gerry Nabarro was a very good-looking guy who was about the same age as me. If he is now Sir Gerald

Nabarro I would not be at all surprised. He certainly knew how to box, and he told us that he was taught at school. Check Gordonstown maybe?

Remember Mrs Grace? Well, she'd decided to head for the U.K. and on her way she arranged that a friend in Estoril send a mandate to me for a fair bit of money, which I received and cashed via our camp interpreter. Her friend was the Princess de Bourbon who was living in Portugal at the time, and wrote me a nice card to go with the mandate explaining the situation. I also found out from earlier correspondence with Mrs Grace that, if you are a 'Lady', the Christian name comes first, like 'Bridget, Lady Barclay' for instance. I did not know that. Every day I learned something from somebody, which I tucked away.

Lots of things happened in Fort de la Revère during our stay there. The food parcels were coming OK now, along with cigarettes and all kinds of goodies. I got a food parcel from my cousin Jean in the U.S.A. but some things were missing. I had also written home to ask if they could send shoes and my mother sent me beautiful cream and brown brogues which I immediately tried to change colour with black shoe polish.

My folks were notified that I was missing and the allotment that I'd made to my mother from my army pay was stopped. Later, after getting a letter from me, which she had to send to the war office along with some kind of proof that I had actually written this letter, the allotment was resumed.

They also had a letter from the War Office that I was on my way home and had been issued a rail pass to Scotland. This would be about the middle of the war. We always wondered who it could have been.

Also in this period, two piano accordions were given to the camp, and it was decided that two people should take possession of them so auditions were arranged and there was one Scottish guy who could play Scottish music, so he got one, and I could play *'Whispering'* with all the correct chords on the piano side so I got the other one.

With me putting up the biggest share, and the rest of the guys in our room chipping in, we bought a short-wave radio which allowed us to a) listen to the BBC and b) catch up on the newest pop music from Blighty.

As the major shareholder, I was in charge of the radio, and I kid myself that I raised the guys' appreciation of music because of this. They would hear something announced and immediately ask me to change the station but I knew this music and said,'Hold on, you all know this', so they got to trust my selection of station.

The Fort was originally built to counter invasion from the sea and we were told that there were naval guns at a lower level reached by elevators and that a large part of the Fort had been closed off, including the rooms where the shells and other armaments had been kept. There was a large tunnel leading from the parade ground into this closed-off section, which had been bricked up, and they also created a wall blocking off the catwalk around the Fort where sentries walked at one time. Fortunately they built this wall round a corner which was right beside our room and although we in our room did not know what was going on, some of the guys realised that you only had to get under this wall to reach the continuation of the catwalk. This position was visible from the top of the fort looking down but only if you were directly above the rooms, not from the other end of the catwalk where the guardroom was.

So, the guys got a blanket down in the shade beside the wall and got the card games going, then positioned a man up on top where the guard might be and if he approached the edge where he could look down he would signal. By sliding blanket and cards away from the wall, they dug down through the concrete and under the wall. This was the shortest tunnel in any prison camp ever known.

I have to digress a little now. Ken was still with the cookhouse group and in another room so we didn't see so much of each other and, because we all had muckers, in the bed next to me was another Scotsman called Alex Ramsay and on the opposite side was another pair I was friendly with, Alf Hendrick and another guy. Alex (Black Watch) was not the brightest guy in the world but we got on OK together. Alf, however, was Jewish and had been a tailor (actually a jacket maker, pants are a different guy) and I'd watched him putting collars on army shirts using material from the tail of the shirt. I'd realised that the collars didn't look too good because they needed to be designed, so I designed the collar and we tried it out. Now we had a smart looking collar and we became the recognised collar maker. Alf taught me how to stitch as a hand stitcher would and gave me other tips.

Back to the tunnel. The guys who dug the tunnel reported to the officers because it was known that they had information on the 'scheme' which was the name given to an organisation that would help escapees. The officers then decided who would go through the tunnel, RAF first.

The great escape began early evening and the guys were going out one after the other. At this point Alf and I decided, 'To hell with this,' and quickly got dressed in our escape clothes, waiting on somebody chickening out. I gave all the food and my accordion to Ken to keep in case we didn't make it out. As I suspected, there was a lull in the sequence. After all, if the guard up above looked down, he was going to shoot.

So I said, 'Let's go!' and off we went. We knew the system by this time. You lay on your back with your head down the hole then got your hands out to the other side of the wall and pulled yourself through.

On the other side, the entire walkway was filled with barbed wire but, being already on your back, you lifted up the barbed wire as you crawled. I was in the lead and the other three were behind me. I could still see the last guy to go before us and we just kept on crawling until we got past the wire.

We knew that a rope had gone out right at the beginning to get down into the moat. However, by the time I got to where the rope was, it was broken, but I knew I could drop from the broken end OK.

Then I had to wait till the other three got to me and, by that time, the guy ahead of me had disappeared. It had been our intention to gatecrash the group ahead but we could neither see them nor hear them and it was beginning to get dark so we had to move on and we decided not to head for the sea where we knew the others had gone. This is where Prince Rainier comes in because we knew he had something to do with how the guys were going to get back to Blighty.

Well, we were on our own now and the only thing I could see was to head right back to St. Hippolyte where I had a good contact, so we decided to head inland, get up in the mountains, circle round Nice and then back to the coast and the rail line.

That first night we were walking on a road behind the Fort and we saw two bicycle lights approaching. I immediately dropped into the ditch at the side of the road but the other three went scrambling up the hillside, making a lot of noise in the bush.

The two gendarmes heard all this commotion and stopped, got off their bikes, shone flashlights around and saw me. I stood up and one asked me who I was so I told them where we'd come from. The other one was threatening to shoot up the hillside but his partner asked me to call my comrades and tell them to come down, which they did and we had a little talk.

At that point I thought that that was it because there were two of them, which would make it dangerous to let us go, but they must have known each other really well because after asking me if I had a knife, and telling me to use it if anybody else tried to stop us, they did let us go. The one I was doing all the talking with even told me his name, which I have never forgotten – it was Pernod, like the aperitif.

After that it was walk, walk, walk, up to the crest of a mountain and down the other side, then up another one. We did sleep sometimes. Two funny things happened on this hike. The first was that as we came to an intersection up in the mountains, with not a living soul in sight anywhere, there was a kid selling ice-cream, so we all bought some. We wondered how many customers he hoped to get – there was not a building anywhere around.

The other thing was that one day, again when we were high up, a thunder storm came up and the rain started to pour. A few yards from where we were there was one of these buildings you find up in the mountains, no windows or doors but it did have a roof so we went in. Right behind us three men came in, then an old lady with a bundle of firewood. The other three, who could not speak French, started talking in English before I could stop them, so the three guys knew we were not French. The thunder and lightning is right above us, being so high, and the rain is pouring down and thundering on the roof and the old lady goes to the door and sticks her hand out to see if the rain has stopped. We all started to laugh and one of the other men turned to me, because I'd spoken a few words to him about the weather, and explained to me *'sourde muette'* with hand motions. Well I knew *'sourde'* was deaf and guessed *'muette'* was 'dumb' from 'mute'. Maybe you had to be there to appreciate the humour.

We ultimately figured we'd got around Nice and it was time to head south, plus there was a wide river bed although the river itself didn't seem very wide. We got down to the main road going west from Nice and headed west but as we got near the bridge over the river, we could see a roadblock on the bridge with traffic being stopped so we had to go back up the river till we could see a place that we might be able to cross. We waited there until it got dark, stripped nude and, holding our clothes high, got over to the other side.

I remember we were all soaking wet but we reached an empty warehouse and I found a piece of canvas and I rolled myself up in the canvas, leaving my clothes off. That is when I found out that if there is not too much air to breathe and you are re-breathing your own breath, the heart speeds up, the body temperature rises and you dry in no time because it is only your skin that has to dry. Don't put on wet clothes.

Next day, we were on our way again. We planned to keep going west then head south between larger towns to find the railroad. On the twelfth day, we were walking through a small town in pairs, Alf and I in front. Th other two were quite a way behind, when I heard someone shout, *'Arrêtez vous ou je tire!'*, 'Stop or I'll fire!'.

We ignored it and didn't turn around, so they repeated it and at last we turned around and two men in plain clothes had the other two. The two detectives had their suspicions about Alf and me but the other two gave the game away because as the 'flics' told us later, they were wearing British army boots. So we were under arrest, taken to the police station and the same afternoon were taken by bus down the mountain to the main road to Nice and by evening were back in the Fort and in jail for sixty days.

We were the last to get caught among the twenty-eight who got out. Sixteen were back in jail and twelve were never seen again. They, so rumour had it, were helped by Prince Rainier and were taken off by submarine. They were mostly the RAF group who went through the hole first. I made a vow then that if ever I escaped again it would be on my own. Before you feel too sorry for us doing sixty days, let me explain what happened.

First of all, because there were so many of us, they

gave us one of the rooms the same as we had been in, with a guard on the door and two exercise periods with only a watery soup twice a day. If you remember, I'd given Ken my store of food before we left, so he was able to get some food into the room by, for instance, slicing up a tin of meat loaf and putting it in an empty carton that a bar of Canadian chocolate came in, so that it could be kicked under the door while the guard was distracted.

Some of the others arranged with buddies to have stuff dropped into the soup, which had to be rescued real quick. One time there was a bottle of wine in the soup but because of the heat, the cork popped out. Every little helped. The large biscuits that came in the Canadian food parcel could also slide under the door – we always knew who the stuff was for from communications during exercise period.

Then to further improve the situation, after less than two weeks, they told us that jail was over and we were being moved to a new place which we were told was Val d'Isère. We moved back to our old rooms for a few days while everything was packed for the move. I got my accordion back from Ken and an illegal six inch diameter hot plate we had and my good four inch locking blade knife was put inside the accordion along with several other knives and we were ready to go.

Before I leave Fort de la Revère, I should say it was rumoured that the German Commission said this large an escape could never have taken place without help from those who were guarding the prisoners, and that the Commandant had been shot.

It was also my introduction to scorpions, praying mantis and other crawling things, and experiencing the Mistral, which was like an air raid when it came up, whistles blowing, guards running all over and everybody locked in their rooms. We also had some new arrivals while we were there, three guys who had got to Switzerland but like us were interned and would have to stay there till the war finished so they decided to try a route through France – it didn't work.

Also, some others arrived, the turbaned kind. One was a Non-Commissioned Officer and the other two were his slaves. They demanded a separate room and had to get special Red Cross parcels for Indian soldiers containing their ghee. Yes, we were racially prejudiced.

Dave in Fort de la Revère
wearing a gift outfit from Mrs Grace

11.

Val d'Isère

In about a year and a half, we will come to another knife story, this time in Germany.

In the meantime, life went on, but in Val d'Isère. About the only thing I remember about that place was that I got toothache and asked the French Medical Orderly to pull out the problem tooth. He had the tools but no cocaine, so I told him to pull it out anyway but he would not do it. My brother George would have done it.

Instead, the Medic gave me a morphine injection which was supposed to make me sleep. I don't suppose you have ever tried to sleep in a barrack-room full of guys who didn't give a shit if you died. All that happened was that I was sick and finished up with a headache that made me almost forget the toothache. I seem to remember the dentist showing up the next day and taking it out.

As it was mid-winter, there was very little talk of escape so we just went along doing what we did, eating, brewing up on my little hotplate hooked into the wiring with two safety pins, playing card games and chess, then early one evening we were told to get ready to move right away.

I can remember walking quite a long way, then finally getting on a train and realising that we were now being guarded by a different bunch of people. This was an ordinary train and it was already night so we could not see much. All I wanted to do was sleep till we got to where we were going so I climbed up onto the luggage rack, took my boots off because my feet were very sweaty after the march and went to sleep.

Day-light should have arrived when I woke up but it was still dark and my feet were frozen. Suddenly it was daylight as we exited from the tunnel and my school geography started to operate especially when we got to Torino. Now even I knew this was Turin so we were in Italy and the only way we could get there was through the Simplon Tunnel. I didn't know then that the pass and tunnel rose to 2,000 metres and that I'd got frostbite on my feet.

When the train finally stopped, we were not in a station and we had to jump down to the ground. I had no feeling in my feet and collapsed to the ground. I managed to get up and we all started marching somewhere. As circulation came back to my feet, so did the pain, but we kept going and reached PG 73.

This was a very large prison camp with a road up the middle and a compound on each side which, we later found, contained two thousand men in each. When we were all in the road with our possessions, they searched everybody. The only thing they got from me was quite a few French francs, I think about three hundred, for which they gave me a receipt. In order to get as much as I could inside the accordion, I'd removed the reed blocks and carried them in my kit. I told them they were spares and they accepted this – they must have thought I was too stupid to open up an accordion.

While the search was going on, we were talking, or rather shouting, to the guys inside the compound. They wanted to know where we'd come from and we told them. They asked if we had any news of the war and we said we'd been listening to the BBC up until the day before when the eighth army had been advancing in North Africa. They came back with, 'The eighth army is in here – all four thousand of them!' Finally we got into the compound and were allocated a whole room to ourselves, all two hundred, where we all grabbed beds. They were double-decker four-plexes. Ken and I grabbed two top bunks right at the far end door, Alf and his buddy were beneath us and Alec was next to us. Ken, no longer being with the cookhouse group, rejoined me.

I assume the reason for sending us to Val d'Isère was that there was an ex-army barracks there which only needed some barbed wire and outside sentries to reinforce it. Also, it was close to where we got aboard the train for Italy, which was all figured out long before we got there. Neither the Germans nor the Italians wanted two hundred trained soldiers around in France in the event of a USA landing on the south coast, which even then seemed a possibility.

By the way, my feet ultimately got better but I could hardly walk for a week, and some parts of my toes turned black. These eventually came off – the black bits I mean! – leaving no sign of damage.

12.

Italy

Now Italy: there are several things I want to say before going into the real story. First, nobody believed our story of semi-starvation. They could not see how we could be so fit, playing football and basketball and walking around the camp in only our uniforms, while they were crawling around in their greatcoats, starving to death. The medical officer examined us and we told him we'd existed for months on half of what they were getting here, and knew how low you could go and still live and function.

I had my accordion and the first night in the camp we had a concert in our barrack-room and we had a few good singers, a guy who could do a take-off on Hitler, and several other acts that we had put together in France. Within minutes of getting the concert going, the place was full of guys from the other barrack-rooms. Over the next few days, the camp changed completely. Greatcoats were off and football games organized, and around the camp it was, 'When is the next concert?' Looking back that is what it seemed like, but it probably took a little longer.

The Red Cross parcels were coming regularly, one

every week, and the food we were getting from the Italians was more than we got in France, not counting food parcels. Remind me sometime to tell you the contents of the UK parcels and the Canadian parcels, no problem remembering that. The next thing to keep in mind is the supply of 'materials', lots of tin, cardboard, string, hot melt glue and solder from the tins. So, one could make things.

For me personally, there were two accordion players who I got friendly with. The first one was Reg Blair.

He said, 'Dave, you know all these melodies but you can't read music, so we can short-cut a system where we break each song into bars (16) and I tell you the chords to play on the bass-side.'

Every day I told him the names of tunes I knew and he would be back the next day with all the chords. A normal pop tune would be 16 bars for the intro, 16 bars a middle bit and then the last 16 bars. If you have ever seen pop music with the guitar chords above the lines, that is what I play.

The other accordion player was Nat Green who would play my accordion so that I could see what could be done.

Not long after we arrived, some instruments showed up compliments of the Vatican: two full size accordions (120 bass), a violin, and a trumpet. Well, obviously, my two friends got the accordions, then a trumpet player came forward who was very good but he could not read music either, and it was a B-flat trumpet, so everything he played was in the key of B-flat, which to this day is my favourite key.

Before very long, we had a little group including a swing violin player. Although I was not yet good enough to join the group, I was a member of the concert party as the accordion maintenance man. If any of the reeds went a little off, I could melt a little wax on the tip then scrape some off until it matched the other reeds playing that same note. There are usually four reeds per note.

We also had another person in the group, Trooper Frank Kennard, who claimed to have conducted the orchestra at the London Palladium and there was no reason not to believe him. He arranged the music along with Reg Blair who wanted to be a music arranger when he got back home. The Italians gave us a rehearsal room where we didn't bother anyone and provided wood so that we could build a stage in the open air. It was also used for what we called 'lectures'.

Remember that with two thousand people, you had people who could do practically anything that was required. A typical lecture could be 'Life in Wormwood Scrubbs' or a Regimental Sergeant Major who was regular army and had been in India and other places, and finished by saying, 'If you can find an easier way to make a living let me know.'

You can see what we started. It was also one of our bunch who, using string from hundreds of Red Cross parcels, produced nets for volley-ball and basket hoops. A double bass also showed up from some place and we found a player for that.

When I say I can't read music, that is not quite true. I knew how to read music but never got past the struggling through bit. Frank Kennard told me that when I got home I should buy piles of music from second-hand shops and start playing, but as soon as I was playing because I knew the tune and was not reading the music, I should tear it up, throw it away and stick up another piece.

We managed to get the score of 'New Moon' (Sigmund Romberg) and got that to the stage where we could perform it to our public, with some of us playing by ear and memory and all tunes transposed to B-flat by Kennard to suit our trumpet player. If we just had to have a change of key in the middle of some thing, you dropped out until it got back to the original key. Enough about music, although it was a daily thing.

Every day we got a little loaf of white bread, about the size of a breakfast roll but with a harder crust, and with the addition of marmalade or jam, which came in the parcels, also marge or butter. It was necessary to have something to cut with so I designed a replica of a table knife, which I made from tin.

I had a strong pair of manicure scissors which could cut tin and the knife blade (thin tin) was backed along its length by a reinforcing piece, and extended into a handle which I folded over, then wrapped another piece around that of a different colour tin. Other than the wraparound, the rest was made from one piece.

Around this time other tin-bashers got into making small hinged lid attaché cases by joining sheets of tin together using the approved method of solderless joints. This seemed like a good idea except you had to scrounge the rubbish dump for clean tins. The brown-coated biscuit tins were the best and they were clean and dry.

I didn't want to go hunting in the garbage and a lot of people wanted my knives so I told them I needed three biscuit tins to make a knife. That gave me two profit so I could make my own case without going to the dump. The cooks saw the knives and wanted to know if I could make one the size of a carving knife, so I said I could try if they could get me bigger clean tins which they did. I made about half a dozen and charged an extra baked onion for each one, which Ken and I shared. The baked onions were a part of our daily diet for a long time.

Another thing I got into was copying cap badges for anybody who had one for me to copy. The outside shape was easy but to create depth I used a nail and the top of my wooden bedpost to punch out what looked like the real thing from the gold coated tins. I could not do the printing of course but I could make it look like the printing was there. With two thousand people in the camp, there were many doing their own thing and the camp organised an arts and crafts exhibition.

If you are saying, 'Dave is pretty good at finding ways to make time fly by', you should have seen some of the things that were in the exhibition. I was just an amateur.

There were birds from wood with individual feathers glued onto a wooden body. The feathers were made by supporting a razor blade flat above a board and then carving a piece of wood about an inch thick with the feather-shape around the outside, then sliding this along the board, taking off a very thin wing copy with each slide. For different feathers you carved the required shape – small feathers or tail feathers. The finished article was beautiful, and that was only one of the many handicrafts.

Because Ken and I still had our little electric ring, we could brew up any time we wanted, but the others were not so lucky and wood was in short supply. This is where the blower was invented although we were told it originated 'up the blue' as the North African desert was called.

The blower consisted of a fan box and a handle to drive the fan, using a speed-up pulley wheel system pushing air from an opening in the fan box through a short tunnel and up through the fire box, very like a little blacksmith's fire. With a little wood or charcoal you could heat a dixie of water in no time. Now this was fine as long as we stayed here but if we moved somewhere else you could not cart these things around with you, so I designed and built one that could be dismantled in a few minutes and packed flat. Just another thing to set your mind to.

Then one day, one of the guys came to me for advice. He told me he was building a cinema organ, (not a model, this had already been done for the arts and crafts,) and he'd built a bellows system and created pipes from tin and inserted mouth organ reeds. The pipes were inserted into a box and all the air from the bellows went into this sealed box.

Right away I could see that this guy was a little bit of a nut but I had to admire the effort, so I stripped down my accordion and showed him how the reeds were mounted on blocks, and the valving system from the keyboard, and also told him that his system would work with a single note at a time but if he tried to play a chord (what's a chord? he asked) he would be out of air instantly.

I thought I'd got him off my back but he was back the next morning, telling me, 'I worked all night on the things you told me to do and could you come over to my place and tell me what to do next'. Very shortly after that we were whipped into Germany, so I never did find out how it worked out.

There is one other subject which I have avoided so

far and that is sex. In France, there was a lot of kidding around, but to the best of my knowledge there was no activity on this. Besides, there was very little privacy. However, in Italy, with two thousand men, it soon became common knowledge that this was going on in a very small way, and we knew most of the people involved. The reason I am bringing this up is because one of the 'ladies', called Jimmy Thompson, loved music and dancing à la Fred Astaire and if I was playing my accordion, sitting on my upper berth in my shorts, and Jimmy came in to listen and request certain tunes, he would place a hand on my thigh. It was exactly like a woman.

'Keep playing, Dave,' I told myself, 'and maybe she will go away…' In actual fact, he was a very nice person and knew his music.

Nat and I would go up to the rehearsal room sometimes and in would come Jimmy and he would dance as long as we played. Nat would do most of the playing with me coming in when I could but we both enjoyed watching Jimmy dance.

Obviously we got him in the concert group doing lady parts, but there was another one named Trixie and they loved to dress up. Alf was still beside Ken and me, and we got him onto dressmaking. Trixie always looked like a guy dressed up but Jimmy looked like a girl. Don't go thinking about how this affected me, it didn't, but I can certainly see how it is; there are certain people who should be female and others who just like going the other way.

13.

Germany

We knew something was up as we could see the Italian Guards running around in circles, including the officers. It didn't take long to find out that Italy had quit the war and then the rumours started. The British had landed and were advancing up Italy and had nearly reached Rome. They had also landed further up and were heading inland, so the Italians were abandoning the camp and getting out.

The guys were talking about going over the wire and what to do next when we heard traffic in the distance and a little later could see vehicles with artillery behind them, and tanks and trucks. They were all backing in towards the camp so we figured that our guys were out there somewhere, but at the last minute they all swung around to face the camp and we were surrounded. Suckers.

The next day we were all marched to a railway station. I remember being loaded onto the cattle trucks (our first time) and going for a long distance that whole day, with only the food and water we'd taken with us. I didn't want to take the accordion with me as I knew I could not march a long way carrying it. Another guy wanted it so I gave it to him. We finished up that night in a marshalling yard in Balzano in the middle of an air raid, and everybody hoped that they would hit the Germans. We didn't care at that point if they hit us.

The next day, we moved into the Brenner and somewhere, I think near the border, they let us out, and we wandered around for a while. I know we got water and perhaps something to eat, and then off we went again right to Innsbruck.

Once again, we ended up in a marshalling yard where lined up and paraded one at a time before German officers and interpreters who asked what our civilian occupation was. I can't remember what I told them but I know it was something stupid like treacle-bender.

I never saw Ken again after that, until after the war, when he visited me in Southsea with his wife (the same girl as before the war). He told me he'd been attached to a German Depot, where he looked after their vehicles. He was very popular with the soldiers, who wanted favours from Ken regarding their vehicles, so he did all right foodwise. He wanted to make sure that I would keep my mouth shut as he'd been doing something he was not supposed to do. He was completely on his own in this position so what could he do? Refuse and get shot. No way.

Meanwhile, I was left in a group of about a hundred, including Alf Hendrick. Alec Ramsay was gone and also Alf's buddy, so we paired up and the next stop was in a transit camp somewhere on the Rhine. We had travelled along the river and looked out of a little window that Alf and I had grabbed in the cattle truck. We saw little mountains that seemed to go straight up out of the water. They were low enough to have mixed forest, not just firs, and they had miniature castles on top.

The transit camp had been converted from a lot of long stables where artillery horses had been kept at one time. Four-tier shelves had been installed where we all had to squeeze in, and it was some squeeze. If you had to get up to go to the trough, you could only get back in by lying on top of somebody and sinking down. This was pretty rough but every cloud as they say...

Alf went outside to get a little fresh air and came back with a hunk of bread. 'How the hell did you get that?'

'I got it from one of the guards.'

You remember that I told you that Alf was Jewish? Well, he could speak Yiddish so he found that he could communicate with the Germans, and boy, did this ever pay off in the next year.

One of the buildings in this camp had been burned down. We were told by the Russians, of whom there were many in the camp, that the prisoners in that building had rioted. The Germans had sent in the dogs, which the Russians had killed and eaten, and finally the Germans burned down the building. We were able to talk to the Russians and that is when we found out that we were not all prisoners together.

They hated our guts because we were all capitalists. When we tried to tell them we were the same as them, they just pointed to our wrist-watches and said, 'Capitalist' and that was that. Back then, they were all so steeped in propaganda that you could never talk to them sensibly.

We moved on from there too and we landed up in a small camp near a place called Immendorf right in the middle of this huge complex which came under the name of Reichswerk Herman Goering. We'd been peddled to a contractor named Karl Plinke, who was building railroads and bridges in the area. It so happens that we were near Wolfenbuttel where my brother George and his wife Nettie were stationed for a while after the war, when my Mum and Dad visited them.

In the other direction was Salzgitter where the iron ore, which fed this giant complex, was mined. Manufacturing proceeded in two directions, to Brunschwieg and the other leg to Hannover.

We landed in this camp on Christmas Day, 1943, with nothing, and not expected, so there were no rations. We swore that day that we would have a proper Christmas Day the first chance we got, and ultimately we did. I will tell you about that later.

We had some Non-Commissioned Officers, including a couple of sergeants, who took over one of the huts along with a few brown-nosers. Alf and I were in a hut with another eighteen guys on double bunk steel beds, four in a group. Alf and I both had top bunks. We were there to work, having been hired by Karl Plinke, and we were paid – in useless paper scrip – but there was nothing to buy.

I got into a gang which was laying temporary railway lines. The work consisted mostly of using a shovel, carrying sleepers or sometimes railway lines. This was the middle of winter and we were fairly low at the time. The ganger, Fritz, was dressed in many layers of clothing and seemed immense, so that you were inclined to do what you were told or get booted up the behind. It was hard going, but along came Red Cross parcels and Spring, and with all the work we were doing we were getting fitter every day. Then came the day when Fritz took off his winter clothing and many of our guys were a lot bigger than he was, so he learned not to push his weight around.

Our part of this work camp was completely surrounded by fencing, but the other part of the camp where there were other workers, mainly Ukranian girls, was open. The first day we went out to work, we all got on this little train which took us up the line to where each different gang was going to work and of course the girls greeted us with *'Dobra ootra'* to which we responded, 'Up yours', or something close to that, which they took to be our 'Good morning', so the next day we were greeted with 'Up yours'.

This was January and these girls had so much clothing on, including quilted suits, that they looked like those dolls that bob up again when you knock them over. You only knew they were female by their voices.

Jumping to the first of May which, I seem to recall, was a holiday in Europe, we wondered what the commotion was in the other part of the camp. Guys were up on the roofs of the buildings throwing buckets of water over whoever was down below, including the girls, with lots of screaming and laughing and everybody having a great time. This is some kind of custom in Europe, although maybe more so in the Ukraine and Russia, and signals spring.

The next day, all winter clothing had been shed, the

girls were wearing dresses and drawing wolf whistles from the guys. Finally, they were females again and were hard to recognise as the same people. It really brightened our day. Now we had to decide who was the best looking, who had the biggest pair, and all these other things that make life worth living.

On the job, there were no portable toilets in those days, so you did whatever you had to do, wherever you could, as did the girls. Of course, there were lots of offers to accompany the girls for their safety. By the way, they were mostly the same age as us. There was one who worked in the company office who had the biggest boobs we'd ever seen and that was before implants.

Back again to probably February. We had a new camp commandant who was a pretty good guy. Alf was already installed as the camp tailor and did a lot of work in their quarters for the German soldiers and officers who guarded us. This had a lot of uses as I will tell you later but the main thing was that this commandant came into our room one night with an accordion because Alf had told him that I could play one. So could he but wasn't very good. He asked me to play and then gave me the accordion to keep.

It was an 80 bass accordion (full size is 120 bass) and was still a lot bigger and better than the one I had in France and Italy but instead of being for my own amusement, it became my duty to play the hymns at our own church services. My knowledge of hymn tunes at that time was limited to *Jesus loves me'* and, every Saturday, the guy who was running the services came into our room and sang the hymns till I could play them. This was OK except that, not having music, I had to remember how it started.

I had a few tricks to help me start so that the guys would sing in the key that I'd chosen to play in. On the odd occasion I would completely forget the beginning. 'Don't panic Dave, let them begin,' I told myself. It only needed a couple of words and I was OK.

While on the subject, a few months later Frank Kennard visited us one Sunday with a guard and played the hymns for our church service. He had a good job visiting the various work camps and playing piano, giving a little concert. He was in good shape and doing what he loved to do.

We had another visitor who came walking along the railway line accompanied by a guard and looking dapper in his pressed British battle dress with little union jacks on his shoulders wondering if any of us would be interested in joining the Free British Battalion. We told him where to go in a hurry. In case you didn't know, the Free British Battalion was run by the Germans and wanted British volunteers in the 'common fight' against the Bolsheviks. Their 'officers' came round camps with food and propaganda, recruiting POWs.

The room we twenty men were in had a stove so when we got in from working on the railroad it was reasonably warm once we got the stove going. We were locked up in the room at 'lights out' time but were allowed to take the shutters off the window. There were floodlights all around the compound so it was never really dark. As soon as we came in, we went to the cookhouse with a guard and got a big milk can of erzatz coffee for each room and a loaf of army black bread between whatever number they decided, and that number grew more and more as the year went by. Dividing the loaf was quite a skill which I still use. We took turns doing the cutting and the person cutting had last pick, so you learned quickly. This system was a carry-over right from France.

As we were locked in at night, we were supplied with a very large wooden bucket which was used for obvious reasons. Now the trick here was to be ready to remove the bucket when it was your turn, with your partner, as soon as the guard opened the door in the morning. If you were slow, it got a lot heavier in the next ten minutes. I hope you are following this and realise how complicated our life was compared to your simple life.

As I didn't have my little ceramic heating element any more, I decided to make an immersion heater so that we could make tea (once the Red Cross packages started coming). I got two small tins, one a little smaller than the other, removed top and bottom and carved four pieces of wood which were equally spaced in between the tins, attached one wire of bell flex (which I stole, along with some bed sheets – which will show up in the story later – when we dismantled one of the ganger's huts) to one tin and the other wire to the other tin. Alf supplied the pins, which I plugged into the lighting circuit and it worked like a dream.

The system in Europe is 115 volts so there was no danger. You filled your dixie with water and dropped in the heater and in two minutes it was boiling but the guys said, 'Dave would it be possible to make one that could heat up the empty coffee can and make a lot of tea?'

Good old Dave said, 'Why not?' So I got two cans that were a little bigger and I also decreased the space between the inner and outer, and the big moment arrived.

The guys filled the can about half full and I stuck the pins into the lighting flex and dropped the heater into the can. There was an immediate humming noise and steam was rising from the water within thirty seconds.

Unfortunately, the lights in the whole camp dimmed slightly and guards came running into the compound wondering what was wrong, but, by that time, I'd pulled the heater out and it was a matter of going back to the drawing board. The guys were very impressed and I said that it would be better to boil the water in two goes, so I got two tins with a bigger gap and that worked for a long time.

Another story is rather depressing but I will tell it anyway. One of the members of our gang was a New Zealander called Bob Parks and Bob had a habit of leaning on his shovel like the rest of us, for a little rest except that his hands would slide down the handle until he was on his knees, asleep.

We said he had sleeping sickness, joking of course, but one morning on the narrow gauge line train that took us to the various work stations in an old street cartrailer, Bob was on his knees asleep on the curved outside platform of the car when the engine got to a place where it had to go over a hill. It was a road actually, about a metre above the line. When the engine got over this hump, it took off down the hill and pulled the whole front end of the car.

I jumped clear but the engine went on unloaded and the car kept going down the hill, being on the ground as the car went past me. I looked back and saw something on the track. I knew right away that it was

Bob, who had fallen onto the line and the car went over both his legs.

I immediately called the guard and we went up to a farm which was near to get something to put him on and try to get transport. We got an old door and went back to the track. Bob was still conscious and asked me to 'lift my poor legs up,' so he knew they were gone.

A truck finally showed up and the guard and I took him to Wolfenbuttel Hospital, where I stayed with him for about an hour during which time nothing was done. The guard said we had to go back and there was nothing I could do, and I think they knew there was nothing that could be done. We knew later in the day that he'd died.

Somebody got the idea that the monopoly money which we got for working was no good to us but theoretically it was German marks and stated that, so we collected it all and it was arranged to send it to Bob's parents. We did have the address, which we got from letters to Bob, and we were helped by the camp commandant.

If you are wondering how a lot of things happened to me, it was because I was the unofficial foreman on the gang – a job I didn't want but because I could speak a little German, the ganger always told me what he wanted done. That leads me into another little story.

One day, when we were working on the line, at a spot where there was a road very near, the ganger and the guard had been talking after it was obvious that something had happened up on the road and he asked me to go up there with him. The guard had to stay to watch the rest of the guys and when we got there, we found a dead German Shepherd (alsatian to you) that we carried back to the ganger's hut.

I went back to work but, later, the Ganger gave me a package of meat for my help. The Guard and the ganger had skinned the dog and butchered it. The guard had heard the noise of the dog when it got hit and went up to see what had happened.

Anyway, I took the meat back to the camp and told Alf the story so we decided to fry the steak, which we did, and it smelled delicious. The rest of the guys in the room were drooling and the only thing wrong was that I just could not eat it, and Alf felt the same way. We had no bother getting somebody else to eat it – they all wanted a piece and they said it tasted great.

Things were pretty rough in the beginning when we got to the work camp – not much food and the middle of winter – but once the Red Cross parcels arrived, things improved considerably. Alf was working with me when we started but it was soon known by the Germans that he was a tailor. Some of the guards had come back from the Russian front wounded and, after being patched up, they were sent to our camp for guard duty. Their uniforms were in poor shape and soon they gave Alf a room inside the camp where he could do work for them and also for our guys.

The guys soon caught on that German for 'tailor' was *'schneider'* and putting that together with my name Taylor, I became *'Schneider'* for the rest of our stay in Germany. Even the guards started calling me *'schneider'*.

One day a guard was talking to me and he said, *'Dein Kamarad bis jude nein?'*

Of course, I said no, but they all knew from the

Yiddish accent.

I don't know if you knew this but when we were all called up at the beginning of the war and were issued with a paybook, it contained, among other things, your religion. No paybook was ever issued saying 'Jewish' – it was always something else. We got a propaganda paper once in Germany and one of the items listed all the well-known people who were Jewish or were close friends with Jews, and also remarked that there were no Jews in the British army. Well, now you know why, and it was a smart move by the powers-that-be.

Early on, after the parcels arrived, I was able to do a few deals with the gangers and guards for extra bread but getting the stuff back in was difficult because the officer in charge got to know about it and we were all searched as we came home at night. I could bring a loaf of army bread in, tied to a piece of string and hanging down my back at about waist level under my greatcoat. We were all wearing these in the winter.

When the guard came to check me, I opened my greatcoat and with both hands swept it behind my back, enclosing the loaf while he searched my pockets and inside my blouse, down my legs then on to the next guy. This worked on the odd occasion when I could do a trade.

Then, when Alf got doing his tailoring, he had to go out to the guards' quarters so that they could try on their uniform jackets and trousers while he pinned them for alterations. This was a great improvement as now we could do much better deals and after a while we were the main dealer in the camp, Practically all black market was done through Alf and me. We, of course, made a slight profit on all deals.

To show you how this worked, we had more bread than we knew what to do with, so we were trading some of our own stuff, Alf's and mine, for eggs. One night we were frying eggs on the stove when in walked the commandant of that time, who was a real bastard. He took one look in the stove and screamed *'das eire'* (I think) but right beside the stove was our garbage can and in it was a small container out of the regular food parcel, which had contained powdered eggs. I grabbed it and showed him the printing on the tin. *This tin contains the equivalent of two whole eggs'*. He prided himself on being able to speak a little English and whether he believed it or not, it gave him an 'out' and he walked out.

That same commandant came in one night to snoop around and search our little cupboards. He found the cubby-hole where I kept a few things I'd picked up on the job, including wire and nails, and he wanted to know if I'd built a radio. He got the guard to rip out my cubby-hole and take everything away. That was no disaster but, in all the commotion, he or the guard bumped into the long table that was in the centre of the room and a knife fell on the floor. He looked at the knife and wondered where it had come from, then caught on and had the guard turn up the table.

Under the table were all our knives, which we rammed up underneath when we finished using them. He then went round the whole camp and confiscated all the knives. They were in a box out in the guards' room and Alf was able to bring them back, a few at a time, without anyone noticing, until this commandant got returned to active service, and the new one (who gave me the accordion) gave us the rest.

At this time, two guards would come in after lights-out with a sack full of bread and we would fill the orders which we'd taken from the guys. The going rate for a bar of chocolate was two loaves to the guy but we charged the guards three – same with a tin of Nescafé, which came in the Canadian parcels and was very popular outside.

We could never find out how much the guards were getting, but we were more than doubling our rations for the week by trading a bar of chocolate. Things were going great for our room – we were sharing the profit around and two of the guys didn't smoke, which meant we had cigarettes to trade as well and they were very popular. The end result of all this was our promised Christmas meal.

We decided that it would be for all twenty of us with everything on the table and each of us could take whatever he wanted. This was completely unheard of as everybody was extremely protective of his own ration, but everybody contributed something.

The two white sheets, which I'd stolen earlier, were used as table cloths and Alf and I managed to do a deal with the local baker for white bread. Even the civilians could not get it but we'd managed, so the bread was sliced, there was butter and jam on the table, cigarettes, and we had baked two cakes. The cake recipe was a carry-over from Fort de la Revère where it originated.

In certain British Red Cross parcels there was a packet of Yorkshire pudding mix and in the beginning we said, 'What the hell are we supposed to do with this?' In the Canadian parcels, there was a large tin of 'klim', whole powdered milk, also a large packet of Sunmaid raisins plus a pound of butter and there you had the ingredients of a cake that we could bake in an army mess tin. By the time we had our Christmas meal, the exact measurements were known and, because the pudding mix had a rising agent in it, the cakes turned out beautifully.

Another thing that came from the Fort was: you took a large white biscuit (there was a packet in the Canadian parcel) about three inches in diameter and a quarter inch thick, and soaked it in water overnight. In the morning, the biscuit was more than doubled in diameter and thickness, and had softened. You then fried this in butter or marge and topped it with whatever you had – jam, marmalade or syrup.

You can see that when we were getting regular parcels we were in better shape than the average German. As long as I am on this subject, some of the Canadian parcels had prunes instead of butter and, in Italy, Alec Ramsay and I would soak the prunes overnight, mix up some thick cream from the powdered milk using a plunger type mixer I'd made and this was our breakfast for a long time. It kept us going. (Joke).

The next subject is bombing. We were located in the middle of a huge target area, Brunswick (English spelling), Hannover, Magdeburg, Salzgitter and the Herman Goering complex. We did have a bomb shelter in the camp but we preferred not to use it, and anyway there was no shelter during the daylight bombing when we were working. It was just like shelling – you got to know if you were in danger. In the thousand bomber raids, we could see the planes and we could see when the bombs were dropped. From the direction the planes were travelling, you could guess where they would land. If the planes reached directly overhead when they dropped the bombs, you were fairly safe, except that sometimes one bomb would break away from the trajectory of the rest and appear to travel backwards.

The immense bombs that were dropped at night made a most peculiar noise that we described as 'the gobble'. They were just huge tanks like on a tanker truck and they were dropped where we could hear them. I can tell you from firsthand knowledge that the movies are full of bull.

The sequence is 1. the flash (the bomb is down) then 2. the noise of the bomb falling. 3. the sound of the explosion. If the bomb falls real close, you don't hear anything. Light travels faster than sound and if it is dark you can see concentric halo rings travelling towards you. We never went down into the shelter because there might be somebody in there whose name was on a bomb.

One day, an American bomber was in trouble and he flew low right along the railway line over our heads, dropping incendiary bombs as he went. One engine was on fire and I guess he was trying to fly low to avoid ac-ac fire and maybe get home. Where-ever you looked there were hundreds of little fires burning. We didn't know then that it was napalm. It landed on some of the guys' coats but we quickly put it out. It was like jelly and smelled of petrol so the guys were putting it in their cigarette lighters, which had not seen petrol for ages.

Also, farther up the line, we found some cannister bombs which were banded together. The band was supposed to let go on the way down and scatter the cannisters, which were full of petrol and had a device on top. This device should have triggered the pressurized petrol to come out through a little hose and be ignited. The ganger we had at the time ran his motor-cycle on this petrol and was able to go home for the weekend.

One bomb, which did work, dropped right beside a wooden building where the engines were kept, and only charred the wood. We saw quite a few American bombers shot down. One crew, all dead, were buried near where we worked. I suppose they found them later. It was well marked. Occasionally, we would see a few parachutes on the way down, but the guard would always tell us they were dead before they reached the ground.

By the second winter we were in Germany, the war was no longer in doubt as far as we were concerned and I think the Germans were beginning to realise this. Even though we could have walked away any time, Alf and I didn't consider that, after four years and not much longer to go, it was worth the risk. You stood a very good chance of being shot and where would you make for anyway, so we decided that the most important thing to concentrate on was our health and we wanted to finish this in good shape, so from then on all our planning was to make sure we walked out of this in physically top shape.

Around this time, they came in one morning and rounded up the whole compound and marched us away over into the Herman Goering Complex where we were put to work in a bomb crater. One of these huge bombs had landed in a field but where it landed was where all the buried power lines were coming into the complex. The cables, some six inches in diameter had blown up in the air and stretched considerably, and no power was coming through. We had to dig down to the underground brick roadway and were supposed to re-lay the roadway then get the cables back down. They were curved above our heads, about six of them. The ground was frozen solid and it took all day to get through to where you could dig, using picks, and the next day you started over as it froze overnight.

After a week or so we were able to replace the brick and the day came to get the cables back, with everybody using their weight to get them back down. The small ones were not too bad but the big ones were not easy. Then finally it was time to put the earth back in and that's where Dave supplied the nails that we hammered into the cables as we buried them. I hate to think what happened when they turned the power back on.

They had taken us to approximately the same place once before, where there was a delousing piece of equipment that looked like an old-fashioned steam engine where you opened the door at the front and threw the clothes in, closed the door and let the steam in. As we were also getting showers, we stripped down, tied our clothes together and went into the showers. The water was nice and hot and we knew nothing of what we learned later, so we came out, got our clothes back, and marched back to the camp.

In both directions, we passed another camp full of guys in their striped pyjama suits. They all came to the fence as we passed but we could not communicate too well and the guards would not let us stop. The thing I noticed was that there was not one blade of grass in the entire compound. The gang I was on passed this same place about two months later and it was empty and overgrown with grass and weeds.

On the 6th June, 1944, we were working on a

marshalling yard where a lot of material was being delivered by rail and I saw the engine-driver talking to the ganger and looking over to where we were working. Then the ganger came over and talked to the guard, who also kept glancing in our direction. By that time, we all knew something was up, so when the guard came over and said, 'Tommy come' we knew the invasion had taken place and it was only a question of time.

This was the time when the bombing really stepped up and, although the Germans knew it was over, they thought the V1 and V2 weapons might still be enough to change it around. We knew about the V1's and had actually seen them being transported on top of planes to their launching sites on the west coast. The V2's were being launched from Peenemünde and we could see the vapour trails from where we were. The ganger was trying to tell me about the V1's which he pronounced *Vo-eins* and that the German word *'voreins'* (or something like that) meant 'revenge'.

As far as I can remember, the delivery of Red Cross parcels became sporadic at about that time, and gradually the rations got fewer and fewer, but that must have taken quite a while because I don't remember it affecting Alf and me too much. As part of our aim in life at that time, to survive in the best physical condition we could, we started working on our freedom clothes against the day we would be liberated.

I still had this large American army officer's tunic that Mrs Grace had sent me, minus brass buttons of course, which we converted to two pairs of walking shorts in beautiful olive drab worsted. Alf did the cutting, and I did a lot of stitching. I was pretty good by this time, having been taught by an expert.

There were many signs that the war was ending. One time, three or four guys showed up in the camp, who had been taken prisoner in France (probably late in 1944 because, by that time, we were being severely rationed) and they were trading their bread ration for cigarettes. When we questioned their thinking, they just said the war would not last much longer. Well maybe so, we thought, but they would learn.

As things progressed, there finally came the day when our fighter planes were around and going after anti-aircraft rail guns in our neighborhood. One dove straight at a gun we could see, and we didn't know what happened but he didn't pull out, and went straight into the rail cars, carrying the gun, which toppled off the track and down the embankment.

Another day, this group of dark-blue-uniformed people showed up near where we were working on a bridge and where there were some unexploded bombs which had been collected. I remember one had landed flat on its side and was oval shaped. The men were supposed to dismantle the bomb and we talked to them. They told us they were submariners and had refused to go to sea so they were put on this bomb defusing squad.

It was now early spring 1945 and finally it was the question: is that bombing or artillery? A few days later we knew it was artillery or tank guns. Within days, we were told to get ready to leave the camp and the next day we went on a day's march in an easterly direction. We finally arrived at a railway siding where there were an engine and cattle trucks waiting, right beside a sugar beet factory, where we put up for the night.

Early next morning, I was scrounging around as

usual and found some little potatoes and took them back to Alf. We had lit a fire with the intention of roasting them when somebody shouted, 'Tanks' and somebody else identified them as American. We watched them coming along this road and as they came to a T-junction they turned left and the guys were all screaming, 'Up this way, you are going the wrong way'. Finally, one of the tanks turned up our way, and came into the yard of the beet factory, where the Americans were mobbed.

The guards were mostly running around offering their rifles to anyone who wanted them. One of our guys asked a guard for the time and when the guard looked at his watch, our guy said, 'I'll have that.'

At this point, Alf and I said, 'Let's get out of here', and we got into our liberation clothes and started walking.

The first night we were liberated, we reached a town and in the town square were piled hundreds of guns, rifles of all kinds, sporting etc. and mostly with the wooden butts smashed. However, I managed to find one in reasonable shape and picked it up. We then came to a house where the Americans had taken over. It was a Doctor's house and very nice.

We spoke to a sergeant and we got a room in the house where we could stay the night, then Alf went for a scrounge around and came back with some bits and pieces. The Sergeant we'd been speaking to wanted to entertain his new-found girl-friend and was looking for something to feed her other than 'k' rations, so he did a swap – 'k' rations suited us just fine.

At the first place we came to that had chickens in the back yard, I went in and grabbed one. The people saw us but they were not going to do anything. I had it plucked and cleaned in no time flat and we decided to cut it into pieces and eat it later. We were only interested in getting west as fast as we could go.

We were moving along pretty good and a lot of American transport was passing us going east and they were throwing all kinds of food and cigarettes at us. Then, as we were walking past a factory, this German went in riding a small motor cycle, got off and went into the factory.

I said, 'I'll have that,' and went over to the door, started the bike and Alf got on the back and off we went on our way.

We had only gone a few miles when a truck pulled up alongside us, going the same way we were, so we stopped and got talking. The outcome was that they would take us back to the H.Q. where they were going so we lifted the bike (which is probably what they wanted anyway) onto the truck. They were both black and real nice guys.

At H.Q. they took us straight into the mess, introduced us to the cook and, it being about 10 a.m. he had a breakfast of bacon, eggs and white bread set up for us in no time flat. After our meal, we took off again and reached a small town.

We joined some American soldiers who had taken over a bank. It was a *'spaarkasse'* or something like that. I translated it into 'some place where you put your spare cash'. It was here that we got involved with a blonde girl who knew where there was a truck that needed petrol to get it going, which is what we wanted – some transportation to stop all this walking. Everything was going the wrong way.

I had a look at the truck and it had been converted to run on gas from a charcoal burner. I changed the carburettor back to its original state and got petrol from the Americans with no problem. However, then the girl informed us that she knew where a German soldier was hiding and, because I had the rifle, she wanted me to shoot him.

So, what the hell – we all piled in the truck with her driving. She was a real tough bimbo. She did nothing for me, but she was female and we'd not been this close to one for a while, so we went along with her scheme.

I remember going into a machine shop of some kind where she said that the man was hiding, and we searched all over but didn't find anybody, so the question was, 'What next?'

We told her that we wanted a vehicle and we were driving past this large 'chateau' for want of the German word and drove up to the front entrance, where we all got out and started hunting around. In one of the outbuildings, Alf and I came across this beautiful BMW sportscar with one flaw – no wheels. We figured that the wheels must be somewhere so we started looking in other buildings.

While we were doing this, a person came out of the house, very well dressed but with his right leg in a cast and supported in front of him parallel to the ground. He guessed we were British and we got talking. We asked him where the wheels were and he told us that the Germans had commandeered all civilian wheels and tyres, which we didn't believe but what could you do?

Then he told us who he was. He was the champion tennis star, Von Cramme. I would think that the leg thing was to keep him out of the army. So, our luck was out and we drove back to the bank.

The Americans were pissed off because they had not been able to blow the vault but in the boardroom there was lots of food on the table, including a very large tin of peanut butter. I had never eaten peanut butter and this tasted great – I was eating it by the spoonful. Then we went out into the town to see what was happening.

The Americans had bust into a food warehouse and left it open for the civilian population, who were arriving with anything on wheels that they could load up and take away before someone stopped them. It sure was a busy little town. Then back to the bank and more peanut butter.

You realise by this time what I am going to tell you. I was as sick as a dog, not only that but for years I could not stand the smell, even a tin of peanut butter in a shop window would turn my stomach over.

From there, the next morning, we got a ride to this place where hundreds of liberated prisoners were assembled and after a few hours getting the camp stories, realised that most of them had been there for more than a week and were supposed to be flown out in the order that they came in.

That didn't suit us and we talked two black Americans in a truck into smuggling us out under tarpaulins, which they did and off we went again, arriving in Bielefeld.

We had finally arrived in a town under British control, where a whole factory and garages had been readied for the hundreds of expected liberated

POW's. The first thing that happened was that we were taken before intelligence people to find out if we were who we said we were, and we had to give them our story.

They would not believe that we could be so fit if our story about the rations for the previous month was true. The medical officer also examined us and he would not believe it either. We both still had our army paybooks but there are no pictures in them. They finally took both of us to the showers and deloused us even though we had none, and took all our clothes, including the shorts we were so proud of. Then we walked along the fronts of a bunch of open garages with tables across the entrances and we were handed a complete uniform as we went from door to door; battle dress, shirt, underwear, socks, boots, cap. Two of us on a set-up for hundreds!

We were fed, and over the next few hours a few more came in. We slept in the empty factory, with beds and blankets for a hundred or more, and the next afternoon we were taken to the airport where they were still filling bomb holes on the runway. We got aboard a DC3 with hard wooden seats along both sides, so we sat facing the middle of the plane, and we flew to Brussels, where there were hundreds more of us.

The main thing I will never forget is that I had got over the throwing up days ago and was starving but they explained that we could only get small portions because everybody would get sick. I had to 'con' the ladies into giving me some extra helpings. The next day we were allowed to walk around the city a bit but had to be back by a certain time because we were flying out on fortresses some time during the day.

We got on the Lancaster in Brussels and took off for good old England with everybody standing on the floor of the plane. There were windows and, as we crossed the coast of Belgium, somebody would say, 'Oh look' and we would all dash to that side of the plane. The pilot must have been going nuts. Then, at one point, I happened to look up and realised there was a guy up there swinging back and forward, handling a gun. This brought me back to reality; the war was not over yet, except for us.

We landed somewhere, I think Stanstead, with the band playing every time another load came in. We were now dressed in our newly issued battle dress and the first thing that happened was that you got this powder blown down your neck, up your legs and up your sleeves, then finally we were allowed through this big curtain to where the ladies were waiting to feed us.

After being fed, we were loaded onto transport and taken to a camp where the army beds were already made up for us and all the paper work we required to get home as quickly as possible was lying on each bed, including the papers we needed to sign to allow us to vote for the Labour party in the coming election. Hell – we didn't even know there was to be an election.

I remember hooking up with a Sergeant Bill Taylor and we took off for the nearest pub and proceeded to get back into shape. Because of my weight loss, I decided Guinness was the thing to drink but it was not popular in this pub so the bartender had to bring it up from the cellar. It was so cold that there was no froth so we asked him to put half a dozen bottles in front of the fire to warm up. We cleaned up that lot and ultimately staggered back to the barracks.

Next day we were all set to go home, travel warrants issued and transport to the railway station, and from there to London, where I phoned my Uncle Bob and told him where I was. We spoke for a while and I spoke to Aunt Nannie and said I wanted to come and see them. Uncle Bob was surprised I didn't want to get home as quickly as possible. I said, 'After four and a half years, what's the hurry?' so he came and picked me up and I spent the night with them, telling stories.

The next day I left for home, not the home I'd left in Kennoway but my new home in Methil. This was a good thing because after my parents had moved, I could no longer get homesick in the prison camps as I could not dream up my home.

Home was not as exciting as you would think it would be. My mother was not like she was when I left home – the correct word would be neurotic – and my father had been ill with pneumonia and was only just recovering. The most vivid memory of homecoming is the first night when I slept in my own room and finally had nobody to talk to for the first time in years. It was a very strange feeling but didn't stop me from sleeping, as it had been a long day.

I was home on six weeks' leave and most of my old buddies were not home yet. The local people had a 'welcome home' party for two of us, the other one being a member of our football team in St. Hippolyte, whom I'd not seen for over a year. Every day there was something left on the doorstep by friends and neighbours – butter, eggs, meat, all rationed things.

Remember, I was always thin, but at this point I was just over eight stone and that was almost two weeks after being liberated.

Thanks to all the gifts, I was now putting on a

pound every day for about a month. I stuck to Guinness for a long time, probably because Uncle Bob drank it under orders from his doctor. In fact, I believe he got it under the National Health scheme. I think my first visitor was Nessie, Gladys' sister, and she'd already let Gladys know that I was home, so within a day Gladys, my wife-to-be showed up. I think it was just an excuse to get some leave.

Somewhere in there, Nettie came to see me, already my sister-in-law, and encouraged me to get married as soon as possible. She thought it was great at that time, but she also knew that I would not want to live with my parents for very long. I was out having my usual nightly Guinness or two with a schoolmaster friend of my Dad's in the Beach Hotel when we knew the war in Europe was finally over.

14.

Looking back

I could have done a lot more with my life, and as my son David often says, 'Dad, you could have done anything you wanted to do, you always knew how to do it, no matter what I asked you to do'. It's the old story, 'My Dad can fix anything,' but where I am missing something is in lack of ambition.

After I got home from Germany, all I wanted in life was enough to eat, a warm bed – preferably with someone in it –, and, strangely enough, hot water. I'd seen so little of it for four years. All of these things were easily obtainable without having to exert myself and, luckily, I went back to a job I loved and which became more and more interesting over the years, even after I retired and started consulting with a U.S.A. group.

Cars were my hobby, but not to change them into something different, just to keep them looking like new and running better than the garage mechanics could.

Neighbours used to think I was nuts doing all my own repairs. I used to say, 'Only the dumbest guys in the class became garage mechanics, why would I let them near my car?' The greatest thing in my life now is to repair something that the manufacturer has set up as not repairable, or doing puzzles, crossword or others like Microsoft's free-cell – don't you ever get hooked on this game.

Where do I stop? When I walk in the door at home or after I get married, or when I emigrated to Canada or should I write my own obituary now?

Enough. I'm off to play golf.

Historical Note

Red Cross Parcels

Dave mentions the Red Cross food parcels received in the camps. The British Red Cross was (and still is) a non-political organisation to help people in crisis. During WW2 it organized medical and other care, and trusted to the red cross symbol on uniforms and transport to protect its people and supplies as they went into war zones.

Volunteers in seventeen centres in the UK packed up to 163,000 food parcels each week, with carefully chosen food and items such as soap and cigarettes. During WW2 cigarettes were included in a soldier's pay and were considered a treat, like chocolate.

The food parcels travelled on one of the eight boats chartered by the Red Cross and its sister organisation of St John, known then as The Joint War Organisation. The usual route was between neutral Lisbon and Marseille (one of Dave's stops, in Fort St Jean) and then by train under supervision of The International Red Cross. French and Swiss postal services also distributed the parcels to camps in France, Germany and elsewhere.

Neither wonder it was hit and miss whether starving POWs and internees like Dave received parcels! Or what state those parcels were in. In theory, one parcel was sent to each man each week, containing tins (dried egg, sardines, corned beef, cocoa, biscuits, processed cheese, jam, margarine, condensed milk, pudding, cigarettes) plus ¼ lb packet of tea and a bar of chocolate.

Acknowledgements

With thanks to Davina Blake for permission to include two chapters from 'Past Encounters'.

Cover art: POW image licensed under the Creative Commons Attribution-Share Alike 3.0 Germany Attribution: Bundesarchiv, Bild 183-J27288 / Koll / CC-BY-SA 3.0;
Combat aircraft © studioalef.

Photos courtesy of David Taylor and Jean Gill.

Map of Vichy France thanks to Adam Carr under The Creative Commons License, and the GNU License, adapted to show Dave's journey.

Dave and Jean, Toronto 2008

Faithful Through Hard Times

The WW2 story of Dave's brother George, a Royal Army Medical Corps soldier suriving through the years of siege on Malta, is told in *Faithful through Hard Times* using extracts from the illegal diary George wrote at the time.

The uncensored story of WW2 Malta

Four years
3 million bombs
***Zero Hour Food* approaching**

'*Based on words and feelings recorded at the time, it is probably unique.*' Don Marshall, Military History Enthusiast

The true story of WW2 Malta from an eye-witness account written at the time in a secret diary, a diary too dangerous to show anyone, and too precious to destroy.

Private George Taylor arrived on Malta in 1940 thinking that shiny buttons would earn him fast promotion; he left four years later, a cynical sergeant and a Master Freemason who never said, 'I was there,' without a bitter smile.

Despite the times he said, 'It's me for the next boat', despite his fears that Nettie had forgotten him, George kept the motto of the Royal Army Medical Corps 'In arduis fidelis', 'faithful through hard times' and only told his diary the inside story of four long years.

Now, the truth can be told.

FAITHFUL THROUGH HARD TIMES

4 years, 3 million bombs
Zero Hour Food approaching

JEAN GILL

The uncensored story of WW2 Malta

Extract from *Faithful through Hard Times*

CHAPTER 1.

Every road towards a better state of society is blocked, sooner or later, by war, by threats of war, by preparations for war... war, which is mass murder organized in cold blood.
Ends and Means

Young men died in wars and old men lied about what they had done in them; George had no intention of falling into either category. He was going to keep his head (when all around were losing theirs), do a good job for a short while and return as soon as possible to Nettie. He smiled ruefully. Why the silly girl had joined up herself, he would never know. It had quite spoilt their secret engagement ceremony, him knowing that she was off to play at soldiers. Perhaps he should not have told her so. There had been one of those stormy moments when she tossed her black curls and wondered that he thought so little of her. He hadn't pressed the point; time would do that for him, time wearing the scratchy unbecoming fabric of army uniform, time following the orders of some other girl who could also be better occupied. Follow orders? Nettie? When, one day not too far away, she promised in church to obey him, she would probably cross her fingers. How could he protect her if she tossed her head and went her own way? Nettie was supposed to be at home, safe, waiting for his return, not charging off round the countryside. She could have no idea what real soldiers like him would be doing on a daily basis. Truth to tell, he had little idea himself yet, but it had been made clear during the six months training that he must keep his kit in impeccable order and run long distances carrying heavy weights. Whatever its military purpose, (his being not to reason why), he was on his first visit across the border from Scotland, his first trip abroad, and, for all his wide reading, he hung open-mouthed on the foreign sights.

For centuries, the British upper classes had sent their children on a Tour of Europe at their coming of age; for young men of all classes, the Second World War enforced such a Tour on a scale never seen before. For twenty-two year old Private George Swan Taylor, his Tour started with a lump in the throat. Goodbye to his parents had not stirred by a hairsbreadth from the Victorian restraint which ruled all their relations. The emotional temperature had risen just enough for his father to say, 'Of course, I no longer expect you to repay your university fees, not with this… 'and his slight hand gesture indicated the station platform, crowded with men in khaki, their sobbing women and small children taking what might be a last look. 'It will just take longer,' George had replied, earning a nod of approval. Perhaps George had imagined a flicker of envy in his father's eyes, his Headmaster father who was recalled from his regiment in 1914 because his country needed its teachers. The photograph of his father in his Black Watch kilt stood proudly on the dresser but the uniform had never left for France with its regiment. Or perhaps George was wrong and it had been fear for his elder son, controlled through habit. His mother's 'You will write, dear,' struck him more as a command than a plea, and it had been, as always, Nettie's hazel eyes which showered him with love and pride. Even if she said nothing, her heart was always in her eyes, sparkling as she smiled for him.

'Do I look all right?' she asked him and he regarded her forehead, clear and shining under its halo of fashionably rolled back curls, her red wool coat with a black velvet collar – a present from her sister Jean, who enjoyed spoiling the baby of the family – and he had said, 'You look fine.' That was not enough and she pressed, 'I want you to remember me.' For two pins he would have run away with her there and then, let the army go hang, let Hitler win the war, but the same eyes would not have let him (she would not have loved him so much, loved he not honour more). He understood that about his girl only too well – she was in love with romance itself as much as he was in love with her. All he could say was, 'I'll remember you,' and he had looked away from her disappointment. One day he would find the words she wanted.

The glitter in her eyes spilled onto her cheek as she waved and he watched her through the bobbing heads and shoulders beside him on the train, crowding the doorway. He screwed up his eyes to sharpen his last glimpse. It was going to be a long ... year? Yes, surely a year would do it, earn him time at home, and then back to it, beating the Hun. How his younger brother David had looked at him when he came home for the weekend and said he'd signed up for the full seven, not just for the duration of the war. George told him, 'Makes no difference; it will last that long anyway.' David himself had missed conscription by a narrow squeak, using Uncle Willie's connections to join the Signals and avoid the Infantry, just before George announced his news.

And then there was a train, and men, and endless physical drill, turning left on command, right on command, eating to command, yes sir no sir three bags full sir until you even breathed in unison. Basic bodily functions were an act of anarchism, surprising you with the reminder that anything, other than your rank, could be private, that anything could be beyond army control. When he signed up with the Royal Army Medical Corps in September 1939, George left a Chemistry degree course at the University of Dundee for a different sort of higher education. If he were honest, he had been restless, not convinced that he was cut out to be Mr Taylor, the Pharmacist, for the rest of his life, even with Nettie beside him. Instead he was becoming Taylor, regressing to the relationship with officers which he'd had with his high school teachers, remembering how to disappear into safe insignificance, doing what he was told. Too many Scots for him to become Jock or Haggis but he supposed those too might become an option. George was ceasing to exist.

Despite the confusion of a heavy snowfall, marching orders, a lorry and another train took the men to Southampton docks, where they boarded *the Amsterdam* within an hour, claimed their fifty cigarettes and iron ration, and bunked down, three to a cabin. They were delayed at Spithead from 3pm till midnight, waiting for an accompanying convoy, but safely reached Cherbourg at 7.30 am on the 15th February 1940. George managed a wash and shave in the water trough on the station platform and then forced down some 'stew' for lunch, a slop of meaty mess which made him nostalgic for his mother's cooking. He took up the offer of a visit to see the town with an anticipation which quickly turned to anticlimax. His accompanying officers and sergeant seemed equally unimpressed by the shabby grey buildings and the slovenly air about the town as sour-faced locals reluctantly opened shutters to poorly stocked shops. If this was the Continent, he had no idea why the rich would holiday here. Perhaps David would have made more of it, speaking French as he did, but even he would have had to work hard to charm a welcome. At least George had time to stretch his legs before cramming with seven others of the party into a second class carriage at the end of the train, knowing he was lucky to have that much room as the men had been split into three groups, each looking after a train.

After a surprisingly good night's sleep, George visited the train Cookhouse and was revitalised by two slices of ham and bread and tea. He passed the time when off-duty playing cards or reading his copy of 'Ends and Means', a work he found very much to his own way of thinking. Huxley would have been amused to hear his philosophical work being passed off as 'ways of improving at cards' when George suffered a few pointed queries on his choice of material. It was easier to get on with other chaps if you didn't flaunt your brains too much, very like schooldays.

The French countryside flashed reflections across the pages of George's book, whitening the shadows as the snow thickened, softening trees and fields to rounded silhouettes, icing bridges over broad, shivering rivers. Standards dropped at lunchtime when George faced more stew, but the bar of chocolate at teatime saved the day. There was no drinking water available so the men had to rely on their water bottles and an occasional tea. Before he signed up, George had never really considered what he ate and drank, nor when, but it quickly became the timetable, highlight – or disappointment - and conversation topic of his day. Duty consisted of an hour with four patients in the Medical Room, at 9pm and 3am, allowing George two spells asleep, which terminated at 9am in a mild, rainy Marseilles. Despite the all-too familiar weather, this was more like it, with the sort of bungalows and scenery that might attract a chap to explore further. No such luck this time and the train took them relentlessly right to the docks and the waiting *Duchess of Atholl*, twenty thousand tons of the best of British shipbuilding, from the Clyde, no doubt. This was definitely more like it; hammocks, four course dinners and waiter service – everything the third class passengers would have had – and paid for. Marvellous!

Bolstered by the good food, a fortnight's pay and a ten shilling sub, George found his sea-legs and his way to the dining-room – with only a few wrong turnings, and even they rewarded him with a blue beyond his experience of Leven and Largo, blue to tempt him out on deck in shirt and pants, sunbathing, in February. Even when the seas grew wilder and ropes were put in place to enable safe movement from door to door, the only grey was the accompanying destroyer. Some of the party was detailed as sentries and submarine look-outs but George was free to sway with the roughening sea, rocking to surprisingly sound sleep in his hammock.

Morning brought the usual army routine of inspection followed by an hour's gym but the rumour that they would reach Malta at four o'clock lifted the men through early tea, into full marching orders and standby, keeping them buoyant for the two hours until they finally docked. George later recorded his first impressions in black ink, in his flowing, looped hand with a hint of angularity to digits and each letter 'r', contradicted by extravagance in the tall initial stroke of a 'p' or the additional curling loops on a capital 'W' or 'T'. His makeshift diary was a Stores Writing Tablet of thin lined paper, with a grey card cover.

Darling,

It is due to the fact that one is not allowed to write much that has made my mind up to chronicle to a certain extent the details of my now somewhat varied existence.
Monday 19:2:40

The first sight of Malta from the harbour is wonderful - maybe you have seen it in the pictures ? The houses tiered on the hills all round with arches and semi-tropical trees. Then it began to get dusk and the moon started shining. All the lights around began to twinkle and it added more charm to the scene. About 6.45pm we started to disembark - I can't describe it - all I can say is marvellous and wonderful. All the lights on the hills round about, the moon, the ships' lights for disembarking and the little gondolas sailing around - each with its fairy lamp.

We got to the shore at 7.15pm and were met on the landing at Valetta. We were taken to buses and driven about seven miles across the island to what is known as Imtarfa. On arriving we were given supper and then - after talking, went to bed - and I didn't need to be rocked.

Tuesday 20:2:40
Up at 6am - washed, shaved, cleaned and on parade at 7.15am. Given another Medical Inspection. Breakfast at 8.15am. Wrote a letter to you about 9am and at 10am we were chased out to permit inspection of room. Went across to the N.A.A.F.I. (Navy, Army and Air Force Institute) which is only a minute away and I had a nice cup of tea and two cakes. Came back and laid kit for inspection. At two o'clock the barber walked in and asked if I wanted a hair cut - so I did. It's fine when the barber comes to you! Then we had inspection until 3.30pm and I think I made a good impression. After that we had tea and four of us went for a walk. (Here we do not wear respirators as it is still a peace time station but we must wear belts for protection)

I saw Anemonies in full bloom - tropical trees and do you remember that cactus my Mother had about 2' high - Well! I saw one the same - only it was fifteen ft high ! On our walk we were pestered all the time - boys selling things and begging halfpennies. One man collared us and said he would show us the Catacombs - after about twenty yards, I said I wasn't going and turned back. I had only gone a few yards when another joined me as he didn't want to go either. About half an hour later we saw the other two again and they hadn't gone. He had asked them into a 'pub' first and they had managed to get out of it and leave him. The 'natives' will run a mile if you take off your belt but sticking a knife in you in the Catacombs would be a pleasure. Anyway we got back quite safely at 5.30 pm.

Then I went to the N.A.A.F.I. and bought this writing

pad - then beat a fellow nicely at table tennis and then went to the pictures in the N.A.A.F.I. at 6.30 pm. It was a very good picture and I got back at 8.30pm when I started writing this.

It seems ridiculous, I know, but my face is red as a beetroot with the sun! I wasn't sick on the boat but since I came off it the ground still insists on rocking! We have a wireless in every barrack room; although the time here is one hour ahead of that in Britain.

I think I have done very well for tonight so I will reserve the rest for a later date
Goodnight Darling.

CHAPTER 2

Of the significant and pleasurable experiences of life only the simplest are open indiscriminately to all. The rest cannot be had except by those who have undergone a suitable training.

Thursday 22:2:40

I finished about 6.15 and then went up to the Recreation Room upstairs - two rooms - one billiard room and the other with easy chairs, tables, writing paper, ink, wireless and everything. I played for an hour and a half, - free too ! You can see how everything is so handy here. In one minute you can have food, tea, pictures, dance, tennis, billiards, draughts, ping pong and it's a couple of minutes to the football pitch and the other N.A.A.F.I. There is a terrific difference here too in that there is never a crush as was always the case at Boyce. I think the company is about 90 strong at present but some are leaving at the end of the week. There are always some on duty which keeps things quiet too !

Tonight, walking back from the recreation room in the full moonlight it was really like daylight - although I bet no-one ever thought of reading in it !! Walking along in the moonlight, jacket and shirt neck open, in the delightfully cool air, has a peculiar effect on me - soothing certainly - and surprise at such magnificent beauty. There is but one way to convince you of the truth in my ravings and that is for you to see everything yourself and then I'll defy you to express in words how you feel. Off to bed now ! Goodnight Darling.

No-one wakened them the next morning and George scrambled to the 7.30am parade conscious of his stubble, not jet black like his brylcreemed hair, nor oddly ginger like his tentative moustache, but dark enough to be an embarrassment. He knew his buttons would pass muster as they could easily go two days, but he was lucky to get away without shaving.

Mid-morning, George would break for tea, cake and a smoke at the N.A.A.F.I. and that was where he found that his suspicions about the wake-up, or rather lack of it, were shared.

'Something fishy about this morning business.'

'Some sod thinks it funny to see us hopping around with our pants down.'

'Nothing for it – Spoof's keen. Put him in charge. Least we'll wake up, then.' George had become Spoofer, then Spoof, after a Spoofer Taylor in a boys' magazine. There was hardly a pause for George to accept his new responsibility before all eyes were on their hopes for a perk.

'Now then, Scouse, what can you do for your mates?' Scouse, whose real name George didn't even know, had been placed in the Cookhouse. He grinned.

'Fancy tea in bed, boys? Or at least in your bedroom.'

'Best offer we've had all week.'

'Dress up for us an all?'

'No chance. Time you paid a visit to Straight Street, you randy sod.'

'Oooh, choosy!'

Shorty turned serious. 'Make sure it stays on the QT boys, it's…'

'More than my job's worth,' they chipped in.

'I'll slip a pail up to you, mornings, half five, and evenings, eight o'clock, best I can do – all right?'

'Wonderful. Football, anyone? Three this afternoon.'

The football pitch was probably the only one in existence that was solid stone. Despite seeing cases all week being X-rayed for injuries caused by 'organised games', George couldn't resist joining in, not even when he was reminded to wear his identity tags in case the medics on duty had to sweep him up. As it turned out, a three-all draw with only minor injuries all round, offered a pleasant way to pass the time. And time was passing too slowly.

Saturday 24:2:40
I was told today that I am to be trained as a radiographer so I must be doing all right and be quite suitable.

It is now 6.15pm and I haven't anything thought of for tonight yet. All the other lads are out so I'll pop off somewhere I expect. I am just wondering where you are and what you are doing at this minute. Have you got the initials on the ring? Have you got the photograph? - And how I curse the fact that the censor makes it impossible to write what I think instead of having to fall back on the bad habit of thinking what to write. Love, George.

He had proposed to her in the bluebell wood, where they courted in the springtime with another couple, their friends Joan and Jack. She chose sapphires 'like your eyes' for her engagement ring, which should be uniting their initials at this very moment on the third finger of her left hand. Bluebells. She said his eyes deepened bluer when his heart beat faster. She asked for a photograph to carry next to her heart at all times, and she frowned at his comment that it would become rather crumpled and bathing would be difficult, but he promised to send one all the same. Her image was on its way to him; her image had never left him. At the sudden recollection of her face, he felt an ache which he was too much a man of science to diagnose.

Sunday 25:2:40

Somehow or other I've missed you more than usual, Darling. I suppose it's just that I'm paying less attention to my surroundings and so think of you more. Everybody else is out - away to Valetta, which is 1/- return by bus. You take a horse cab (if you want) for a three mile roundabout road to the bus stop for the large sum of 3ᵈ each. I haven't been in Valetta since the night we came here. To tell you the truth I am spending quite enough without galavanting away 'to town'. I think my average is about 1/3 a day - roughly 2½ᵈ for cigs, 3ᵈ for tea and cake in the forenoon - and the rest for supper. Then I was at the pictures once - 6ᵈ - and I see 'Idiots Delight' is on tonight so I think I will go 'and chase the shadows away!' Anyway you will see that the present rate of expenditure leaves very little over at the end of the week, so it will have to be cut down somehow in order to save a bit. I could do with a pair of light boots - which one is permitted to wear on duty - only they cost 18/- made to measure, so that is out of the question at present..

Today, about thirty men left for home and what surprised me was that they seemed to be going just because they had to and not because they wanted to. This certainly was the case with a few I spoke to, who were absolutely disgusted.

After dinner, I went up to the Billiard Room and played all afternoon. And now I am going to write you a short note for posting, in which will be written as little as possible. I do hope that you do not misunderstand my short, dry letters but I just can't help it.

Love, George

P.S. I was wrong about the price of cigs - it's $2\frac{1}{2}^d$ for ten but I only smoke ten a day anyway.

It was too bad that every word he wrote in letters was not only read but censored; if he so much as mentioned the price of cigs, the sentence was likely to be ripped out as a threat to national security and he could do without the ensuing reprimand, too. He studied the photo he was sending. He looked as bald as a baby with his hair hidden under his cap but he'd seen worse mug-shots. He looked extra spick, with cap-badge and buttons gleaming, but the jacket looked so bare; he hoped it would not be too long before he could add some stripes. Still, his mother and his girl needed a picture of him now and he would not disappoint them. He thought of Nettie at odd moments during the day, predicting what she would be doing, wondering if he was right and how she was coping with their enforced separation. Was she coping too well? He was not allowed to tell her he missed her or anything at all that might give the enemy the impression that British army spirits were vulnerable to any human emotion. He was probably allowed to tell her that he had seen a snake about 18 inches long and three-quarters of an inch thick but didn't know if it was poisonous; he could also tell her that he had seen clouds for the first time in a blue Maltese sky. What would she think of him, talking about the weather – he flung his pen across the bed and went to the N.A.A.F.I. to play draughts.

His spirits lifted the next day when he heard that there was a letter for him – only to drop further when he found it was for a different Taylor, forwarded from Crookham on 9th January so goodness only knew when the other chap would get it. Strange to think of some other man's fragile contact with home contained in this plain envelope; was his alter ego even now looking at Nettie's handwriting?

Then, when he went to wash some hankies after tea, some man washing himself accosted him with, 'Blimey, just the guy I wanted to see – I could twist your neck.'

'Me?'

George recognized the Sergeant in charge of X-ray. 'You're the idiot who posted the Major General's X-ray to him, then?'

'No idea what you're talking about. I dropped in a special report to the hospital office if that's what you mean.'

'Well, the report's missing and the wires have been red-hot all afternoon. There will be some stripes missing in this district if that report reaches the patient, I can tell you, so you'd better hope it's not been sent where the Sergeant in charge thinks!'

George knew better than to point out that he'd just followed orders in passing on the report; he had a fair idea why both sergeants were nominating him as villain of the piece. 'Perhaps it will turn up with the body that went missing out the mortuary.' Caused a fair stink, that had and upset the post mortem mightily. George continued washing his hankies.

Outpatients seemed determined to refer all their clients for X-rays the next morning, including a

Maltese lady whose case-notes queried 'Twins?' in the Medical Orderly's scrawl. It gave George the chance to try out the local phrases he'd been learning, earning shy smiles with his attempts at bonjoo (hello), keef in-ti (how are you) yek yoj-bok (please), gratsee (thank you) and sahha (goodbye). There were three more cases of 'Twins?', one potential pair being so close to arrival that the Sergeant declared, 'If she starts any tricks on my X-ray table, I will really lose my temper!'

'Marvellous thing, X-ray, ' George smiled at the agitated patient and they got her off the premises without mishap and with a confirmed double blessing.

'That report turned up, you know,' the Sergeant told him as they switched plates.

'Really?'

'Returned to the Hospital Office. Been dispatched now – correctly addressed. Man there couldn't organize the proverbial.'

'Mmm.'

'Did I tell you I got a wire yesterday? The bloke at the P.O. says 'Will I read this to you?' so I says 'Go on then' and he reads, 'Solution to all difficulties immediate marriage!' Last thing I want to see all morning's bloody twins!'

'I can imagine.' George could also imagine the laughter in the Post Office and how red the Sergeant's face had been, which was enough to restore their working harmony. This included the Sergeant telling George to 'Scram' although there were four patients. Obedient as always, George scrammed, bumping into the Office Sergeant, also on his way home, and keen to offer George something as near an apology as dammit. So all the little sergeants were quite pleased to keep their stripes as it turned out.

Sunday 3:3:40
Surely it can't be long till I get a letter from you now, Darling. Here's hoping. Love and kisses.

Monday 4:3:40
Some of the lads got letters today so I expect mine will be on the next boat - I hope! Goodnight Darling.

Just as I was putting this away I heard that all regulars are to go home next month! Well! Maybe yes, and maybe no - just wait and see!

Wednesday 6:3:40
Oh! Yes! I got a letter from Kennoway today, so surely yours just can't be long now. Goodnight.

Past Encounters by Davina Blake

'A compelling story about love and heartache and forgiveness and war.' Library Educated Blog

From the moment Rhoda Middleton opens one of her husband's letters and finds it is from another woman, she is convinced he is having an affair. But when Rhoda tracks her down, she discovers the mysterious woman is not his lover after all, but the wife of his best friend, Archie Foster. There is only one problem – Rhoda has never even heard of Archie Foster.

Devastated by this betrayal of trust, Rhoda tries to find out how and why her husband, Peter, has kept this friendship hidden for so long. Her search leads her back to 1945, but as she gradually uncovers Peter's wartime secrets she must wrestle with painful memories of her own.

For if they are ever to understand each other, Rhoda too must escape the ghosts of the past.Taking us on a journey from the atmospheric filming of Brief Encounter, to the extraordinary Great March of prisoners of war through snow-bound Germany, this is a novel of friendship, hope, and how in the end, it is the small things that enable love to survive.

Includes discussion points for reading groups
www.davinablake.co

Past encounters

Some memories fade,
some refuse to let you go

DAVINA BLAKE

Extract from Past Encounters *by Davina Blake, telling the story of Peter, a Prisoner of War*

CHAPTER 21

1941

Peter

Peter was nervous, his empty stomach cramped with tension, causing him to double over, clutching at the griping sensation. There was a mist hanging low over the fields; the sky was grey as ash. He wondered when Neb would make his move. His heart jumped in his chest every time there was a sudden movement or noise – a crow landing by the fence, or the tractor on the farm starting up.

It was coming on to winter again now and they had grown used to the life, physically, if not in other ways. Their arms were weather-beaten, muscled from hard work. Their stomachs had shrunk, but they never became used to the discomfort of hunger; they still felt the need to scavenge in the waste of the produce they harvested.

Peter marvelled that the guards could not sense something – the men's unease, their bodies ready to run or to dive for cover.

He loaded the beets into the barrow. If he could get away with it, he pissed on them when they were in the lorry. Small acts of sabotage kept him going. Peter paused a moment, stretched his back. Harry's eyes were also trained on the edge of the field. It was nearly changeover time. He guessed this was what Neb had been waiting for.

Harry nodded at one of the guards, who in turn raised his arm to another man near the gate to the compound. That man began walking rapidly down the hill and out of sight. What was all that about, Peter wondered?

When it happened, it was so quick there was barely time to hit the ground. Men running, scattering in all directions. Peter dropped fast. It was what Neb had told him to do. It was a split second before the firing began, the ear-shattering rat-a-tat drilling him further into the ground. When it stopped and he heard an engine start, he raised his head a fraction to look. The field was strewn with bodies, but how many were escapees, and how many just terrified men like himself he couldn't tell.

'*Aufstehen!*' The call roused people to stand.

'*Hände hoch.*' Hands up. It reminded him of Judgement Day, all these men rising out of the earth, arms to the sky. Peter staggered to his feet but several others didn't stand. Peter thought they might be alive but in shock. At least he had known it was coming. He flicked his eyes over towards the woodland, saw figures dashing between the trees.

A battery of gunfire, flashes and smoke in the brake of trees. Some men fell, others ran in zigzags trying to dodge the line of fire. It was hopeless; they didn't stand a chance. Someone had tipped them off; they'd been waiting for them.

Guards came to round up the rest of the workers. 'Stand up!' A guard spoke in English. With a flood of relief Peter saw Archie at the other end of the field, but many prisoners still did not stand, perhaps too scared to do so. The guards let rip with machine guns to make sure they were dead. At least one was obviously alive because when he realised what was happening he began to rise, but too late. The bullets caught him in the neck and he jerked. Blood spurted; he clasped at his throat with a bewildered expression, then flopped back to the ground.

'It is a very bad thing you have done,' said Fuhrmann, one of the older, flabby-cheeked guards. The irony was not lost on Peter, who was too angry to trust himself to reply, even if a reply had been called for.

After they were force-marched back to the barracks, Fuhrmann took away their boots and locked the door on their billets. The staccato noise of distant machine guns and the barking of dogs sent ripples of apprehension up his spine. He hoped Neb would make it. He found he was holding his thumbs tight in his fists, willing him on.

Harry was white-faced, jumpy. When Peter touched him on the arm he spun round so quick it nearly knocked him over.

'Did you see Neb?' Peter asked.

'How the hell should I know? Just leave me alone.'

An hour later the message came to line up for roll call.

The temperature had dropped and the cold ate through Peter's clothes, turning his skin to gooseflesh. He wondered if they were going to keep them standing there all night. But no, after forty minutes or so a cart pulled by a bedraggled horse was ushered through the gates. Hauptmann Weinart appeared and ordered Fuhrmann and another guard to drag the English bodies off the cart. They yanked them off by the nearest limb, and let them slap anyhow into the mud. Peter could not see properly, past the men in front, who they were.

The bodies steamed, still warm. There was absolute silence in the yard. He counted twelve bodies. He was willing Neb to have got away, that he wasn't amongst them.

It was a lesson. To show them how many had failed. When he'd been marched back to his billet, Peter was shaking and could not stop. His teeth chattered with it so he could not sleep. He'd called himself a coward because he hadn't tried to escape with the rest. He'd been ashamed he and Archie had funked it. When Neb had asked him, he had been inches away from saying yes. But if he had, he would likely be one of those out there now, face down in the mud.

In the morning they had to march past them to the day's work. Carrion crows flapped on the corpses with their black wings. It was a shock to see some other creatures so close up. They had glimpsed mangy-looking cats and even rats before, streaking past them from the farm. Someone always wanted to trap them and eat them. Peter had the urge to stop, to study the crows' elegant flapping wings, watch their sharp beaks, their bold button eyes, but at the same time he wanted to scream at them and chase them off. In the end he just turned his face away, his fingernails digging into his palms.

Archie was already in the field, unloading spades and buckets from the truck. 'He didn't make it,' Archie said, dumping another spade on to the pile, his gaze flicking to the two guards who were about twenty yards away.

'You sure?'

'Yes. I passed quite close. I recognised his hands. Neb had such big hands.' Peter glanced to Archie's mangled hand. Archie thrust it out of sight into his pocket.

'Poor bugger.' Peter dragged a hoe off the truck.

'Two from our hut went too.'

'Brave lads. I didn't try, because I didn't know if I could.'

'You'd be all right. You're sort of invisible. I mean, you don't stand out. You just look, kind of ordinary.'

'At least it's not an ugly mug like yours.'

'You wouldn't really have a go, would you?'

'Don't be daft.' Peter slapped him on the shoulder. 'What will happen to them? They can't just leave them in the yard, they've got to let us bury them. It's law, isn't it?'

'Don't know,' Archie said, handing him another hoe. 'But I know I couldn't afford to try anything. They're already watching me to make sure I work – because of this hand. And I want to have that drink with you at the King's Head. And a huge plate of steak-and-kidney pie and chips with gravy like we promised.'

'Don't. My stomach feels like it's squeezed dry.'

Another morning of back-breaking work followed by orders to dig graves in the copse for his comrades. Archie wasn't picked because of his bad hand. The ground was heavy with clay and riddled with tree roots. A deliberate choice. In the end they had to send for picks to do the job. After an hour or so of digging in the increasing rain, Peter cursed Neb and all the other foolish buggers who had tried to escape. Escapees just made conditions harder for those left behind.

'Someone must have known they were going. Or how come they'd got men in the trees?' one of the men asked as they walked back to the compound.

'I saw Foster talking to the guard when he was unloading from the truck yesterday morning,' Harry said. 'Best ask him what he was saying.'

Peter leapt in: 'I was with Archie then and I never saw that. And anyway, Archie wouldn't give anyone away.'

'He's unpredictable though, isn't he. That hand injury, he did that to himself.'

A rustle of interest went round the rest of the men. Peter said, 'That's unfair.'

'You saw him though. You were there. He did, didn't he?'

'That was a long time ago, not long after he'd been taken, and he was still suffering from trauma.'

'Suffering from trauma.' Harry imitated Peter's voice. 'Well, I've news for you. So are we all.' He looked round the gathered men for their sympathy. 'So are we all, but we wouldn't give our mates away.'

'How do we know it's not you?' Peter flashed back. 'I saw you nod at one of the guards. You're the one who's in with the Jerries. You shouldn't make accusations without having firm evidence.'

Harry laughed, as if the whole idea was ludicrous. 'I didn't accuse him of anything. Don't start flinging mud at me just because I ask questions. I'm just saying its worth asking him, that's all.'

Peter could not trust himself to speak. He set off ahead of the others, marching up near the guard, until he realised even that might be the subject of speculation. Reluctantly he slowed. Archie knew nothing about it, he'd swear. And he wasn't going to let poor Archie be a scapegoat for this.

***

By the time he got back to camp four of the corpses were in flimsy wooden coffins. Someone had found a flag from somewhere to drape over one of them. Only ten men were allowed at a time to take each man for burial, as the Germans could only spare two guards with dogs.

Peter and Archie were allowed to march Neb to his resting place. Peter was at the head end, but there was no coffin for Neb, just a stretcher. Neb had machine-gun holes in his chest and his uniform was caked with blood and mud, but otherwise his face was expressionless. It was this that was the hardest to bear. Peter wished he could summon Neb back, ask him what he was thinking, where he'd gone.

The wind had risen, and the few trees on the knoll of the hill creaked and rattled. When they got to the site they upended the stretcher to tip his corpse into the hole. Archie and Peter got in with him to straighten him before Peter climbed out to throw the first spadeful of earth over him. It seemed sacrilege to cover his face like that, as if he wouldn't be able to breathe. But of course he'd never breathe again anyway.

'Shall I say a few words?' Peter asked. 'I'm not a

vicar or anything, but we should say something for him.'

'Not just for him,' Archie said, 'for all of them.'

'For all of us, you mean,' said George Henderson.

'Maybe the Lord's Prayer?' Peter suggested.

'Oh no, not that again,' George said.

'Does it matter?' Peter said. 'He's dead. Someone just say something.'

Archie took a breath:

'Half a league, half a league,
 Half a league onward,
All in the valley of Death
Rode the six hundred.'

Archie recited the poem with the noise of the wind blustering behind him. His voice was quiet and they had to strain to catch it, but they were all entranced by the familiar words:

'Forward, the Light Brigade!'
Was there a man dismay'd?
Not tho' the soldiers knew
Someone had blunder'd:
Theirs not to make reply,
Theirs not to reason why,
Theirs but to do and die:
Into the valley of Death
Rode the six hundred.'

He paused. 'Sorry. That's all I can remember.'

The wind dropped eerily into silence. Peter was choked. The words of the poem had taken him back to school, to boys reciting in the fuggy classroom, to the sound of the school bell, the scrape of chairs.

'Neb would have enjoyed that,' George said. 'Bloody stupid. Just like him.'

They laughed then, and the wind rose up to whip the branches overhead, and those with tears in their eyes were able to dry them.

***

Later that evening Archie appeared next to Peter's bunk as he was trying to write a letter home. 'Some men from Neb's barracks came by and asked me what I knew about the escape attempt.' His tone was accusatory.

Peter put down his pen and said, 'So?'

'I told them I knew nothing, but they didn't want to believe me. They said you'd told them I was talking to the guard.'

Peter swung his legs out. 'I said no such thing.'

Archie studied his face as if searching for the truth. 'I can't believe you'd think I had anything to do with it. I didn't know anything, didn't even know they were going. Why the hell didn't you tell me? Why am I always the last to hear of anything round here?'

'Calm down. I didn't want to risk anyone who wasn't involved. I helped Neb with his German papers, that's all, because I speak a bit of German.'

'You could have told me. My German's better than yours.'

'I wanted to tell you, but I promised Neb I wouldn't.'

'It was awful. I didn't know what they were talking about. It made me seem stupid, suspicious. They think I tipped off the guard. They all stood there like some sort of official delegation. They didn't exactly say it, but from their questions I knew that was what they were thinking. How could they think I'd do that?'

'It's not your fault. Harry Tyson set the idea in their heads.'

'Why?'

'Who knows? Maybe Harry wanted to move the blame further away from himself. No, I take that back. That was uncharitable. You didn't talk to a German guard yesterday morning, did you?'

'You saw. You were right next to me. What is this?'

'I know, I know. I just needed to be sure.'

'You mean you don't trust me.'

Peter shook his head, sighed. 'Look, I do. I'm sorry. I'm just on edge, upset. It's been a hell of a day. We all want someone to blame. Harry too. It doesn't mean anything. Everyone's on short fuses, that's all.'

Archie sat down on the side of the bunk, looked at his boots. 'You don't understand. It's bad enough with the work. But the toughest part is not being liked.'

'Don't be so hard on yourself.'

'No, listen. It's true. So don't insult me by pretending it's not. I know I'm not Mr Popular.'

'I think we all feel that way sometimes.' Peter reached out to touch him on the arm. 'Don't let it get to you.'

Archie shrugged his hand away. 'It's all right for you. The men respect you.'

'You're just having a bad day, that's all. Tomorrow it will—'

'Why, Pete? Why don't they like me?'

Peter looked at his earnest face and couldn't

answer. Perhaps it was just that Archie looked as though he needed a friend too much, perhaps it was that they sensed some weakness in him. And despite Archie's pleading eyes, Peter could feel himself recoil, as if even Archie's question was pushing him further away.

CHAPTER 43

1945
Peter

Peter used the wall to claw his way to standing. Nobody wanted to lose their place so everyone slept in the road, heads on their baggage. He was anxious. Archie had barely spoken a word since Annegret and Klara had left, and he must have been up early because he was much further down the queue than Peter. He swallowed. Did Archie really mean to risk it? It would be suicide. Nobody could get past those Nazi guards.

Refugees were still pouring into the town. It reminded him of something biblical, this mass exodus, a whole population on the move. Several trains rattled into the station and out again. The military had commandeered all the trains at Spremberg to send troops to and from the front. The queue compressed towards the platforms.

Archie's head moved further and further away from him down the line as the hours passed. Peter's ankle hurt again, a deep throbbing pain. Several times he almost joined the queue, but he was afraid. It was the same feeling he used to have as a child when he couldn't swim and stood terrified and shivering on the edge of the freezing pool, his bare toes a few inches above the water.

At one point a fleet of army ambulances arrived. There was a clamour from the crowd who hoped the trucks had come to deliver food or fresh water, but no, they were medical orderlies there to meet one of the trains. The train was a freight train of cattle trucks. The German conditions for their own wounded were as bad as for prisoners of war. Troops waiting for the train out were ordered to lug the covered stretchers bearing the bodies of men who'd died on the journey.

It seemed inhumane, this. That the young German soldiers were seeing the spectre of what they, in only a few days, would become. Sympathy stabbed like a needle in his chest. The German youths were white-faced and trembled under their caps. Their new uniforms were soiled with blood as they loaded the screaming men into waiting trucks.

When they'd gone, the crowd moved further down. Terror for Archie made Peter light-headed. He looked up the road. Another wave of refugees. If he didn't move now he would lose sight of Archie and be on his own. Archie wouldn't – he wouldn't leave him behind, would he? Peter craned to catch sight of Archie's head. A ripple of panic overtook him and he limped to the end of the line, just behind an elderly woman with a wrinkled blue-faced baby in her arms.

The clanging bell resounded in his ribs.

A train. In the right direction this time, but only four carriages again.

The crowd surged forward, everyone elbowing and jostling so that he cannoned into the woman in front.

A bag on the old lady's back smacked him in the face as she turned to curse him. Peter couldn't see Archie any more – there were just too many people. The queue stopped abruptly, Peter almost tripped and fell.

Ahead of him there was a disturbance, the noise of shouting and a woman's cries. A rat-a-tat of gunfire. The people behind pushed him like a solid wall. Peter caught hold of the old woman's shoulders and tried to move her aside, but she couldn't move, she too was wedged fast.

'*Entschuldigung,*' he said, trying to squeeze past a man on his left, but he was not quick enough.

After what seemed like only seconds he heard the rhythmic noise of the train accelerating and an audible collective sigh of disappointment.

He stood on tiptoe. He was about fifteen yards from the barrier; there was still a knot of people there, but he couldn't see Archie anywhere.

There was something lying on the track, surrounded by soldiers, but he couldn't see what it was. He stopped a woman coming back from the barrier with a hand on her arm. '*Was ist los?*'

She shrank away from his urgent manner. '*Tot. Keine Papiere.*' She pulled her arm away from him, called protectively to her young son to follow her.

Someone was dead.

Peter fought his way towards the barrier through the hostile crowd. He used all his strength, not caring who he was elbowing aside. One angry old man yelled at him in guttural German. When he ignored it he spat at him, gestured him to go back to the end of the line. Peter knew it was risky to draw attention to himself, but he had to know if Archie had made it on to the train.

He felt someone take hold of him by the waist. Peter turned in anger, to push the person away.

A pair of familiar pale blue eyes anxiously searching his.

Archie. My God. 'You stupid bugger. I thought you were a goner. Don't you ever do that to me again, you hear?' He shoved him hard in the chest. Archie doubled over. Shocked, he stood upright, flinched away.

'Don't. People will notice.' Archie beckoned him away from the barrier. 'You were right,' he said. They shot the man in front of me who could not produce his papers quick enough. It was horrible. His wife and kids were stood there screaming. He was shouting for mercy – Czech, I think. Anyway, a language I couldn't understand.' Archie leaned over, put his hands to his knees.

Peter rested a hand on his shoulder, felt him shivering through his clothes like a dog just out of cold water.

Archie inhaled a convulsive breath and stood. 'I'll be all right in a minute.'

Peter waited, rubbing his back.

'Sorry,' Archie said. 'It just got to me. As if he wasn't worth a farthing.'

'Not worth the risk then. We'll have to try to cut across country. Let's get somewhere we can talk, look at the map.'

'I hope Annegret and Klara are all right. I've still got her case, look.' Archie held up Annegret's suitcase. It was a battered old thing, tied together with what looked like the belt of a dressing gown, the leather corners warped and scuffed with use.

'If we're not going to meet them in Dresden

there's no point in taking it with us,' Peter said.

'There might be something useful in it.'

'Okay. But let's look first, see if it's worth carrying. She won't mind.'

They walked away around the corner of the building, past the long straggling queue, and sat down, backs to the wall. Archie's hands were shaking so Peter untied the belt and opened the case.

'I don't like it, Pete. It feels like spying, to go through her things,' Archie said, as Peter passed a white blouse and a hand-knitted jersey into his hands.

'I know, but they're no use to her. Not now we've got them anyway.'

There was a wedding photograph in a frame in which a smiling Annegret was seated with a bouquet on her lap. Behind her a handsome man in German military uniform stood with his hand resting on her shoulder. Peter gave it to Archie and saw him stare at it a moment too long before he said, 'He must be short, to have the photo taken with her sitting down. Old photographer's trick.' He thrust it at Peter. 'Put it back.'

Peter slid it to the bottom of the case. His hand felt some papers underneath what looked like a pile of school exercise books, a batch of documents all together. Peter picked one out.

'*Deutsches Reich Kennkarte*,' he read. He opened it to see the serious face of a boy staring out at him. Dieter Schönhorst. Annegret's dead son. The same straight nose, same square jaw. Here he was. It was sad to think he'd been so recently alive, a boy still so young his identification card was being looked after by his mother.

Another small square tan-coloured book caught

his attention. '*Soldbuch*', it said, with a logo of an eagle clutching a wreath and a swastika in its talons.

'Look at this,' he said with mounting amazement. 'It's her husband's papers. Karl Schönhorst.'

'But he's dead, isn't he?' Archie scowled.

'Yes, but I think this is his paybook and ID. She's kept it as a memento.' Peter held it out towards Archie. 'How awful. Husband and son both gone, and so close together. But what do you think?' He raised his eyebrows. 'It's got to be worth a try.'

'No. Too risky. You didn't see them gun that Czech down.'

'Let's think it through, weigh it up.'

Archie was quiet for a few minutes, his forehead furrowed. 'Well, I've saved a photo of me and my mother. It might just be big enough for me to do something with. I could take the boy's permit and try and put my picture there instead of his. Pass me the boy's permit.' Peter watched him touch the face with his forefinger. 'He looks like her, doesn't he?' He sighed, braced his shoulders, 'It's possible. I'd have to cut carefully round those rivet holes, though.'

'What about the stamp?'

'Don't know. Suppose I could try to copy it. It's quite grey and faded. It might work. Have you still got your pencil?'

Peter patted his pocket. 'That will leave me with the soldier's pass then.' He looked through the booklet, trying to decipher the German as best he could. 'Oh Lord, I'm pretty sure this word says "deceased" here. What can we do about that? And I look nothing like him. Not to mention my uniform under this lot.'

They ruminated a moment.

'Here.' Archie whipped the book out of his hand and taking it to the edge of the road, smeared mud liberally over the pages and particularly over the word '*verstorben*'. When he had finished it looked as though the pass had been in battle somewhere.

'Hey, that's not bad.'

Archie grinned, pleased. It was the first time he'd ever praised him, Peter realised.

He tried not to show how cheered he was at Archie's reaction. With his pal by his side, life was suddenly brighter. Perhaps even getting home was possible.

He said, 'Shame I can't do much about the photograph. I'd need to be in uniform, so we can't change that.'

'Tell you what, though. I'll bandage you more, over your face.'

'Oh, fine,' Peter said. 'Why don't you just cover me completely like Boris Karloff in *The Mummy*.'

'I haven't got a better suggestion. You're an injured soldier back from the front, right? We'll have to hope they don't look too close.'

'I'm not sure. I've never been much of an actor.' Now he was wary of the idea just as Archie was warming to it.

'It's worth a try. We've had a few lives already. If we can only get to Dresden, Annegret might persuade her mother to take us in whilst we find out what's what. And there's no military bases at Dresden – it's supposed to be full of refugees. Come on, we'll just be two more. And won't Annegret be surprised when she gets her suitcase back.'

***

They were as ready as they were ever going to be. They'd familiarised themselves with the currency in Annegret's bag, and the likely train route to Dresden. Archie's *Kennkarte* was reasonably convincing at a cursory glance. Peter was to go a little ahead as his leg made him the slower of the two. Archie was to try and look as if he was with a family, so the pair of them would not be so obvious.

It was twilight by the time the train came. Peter limped towards the barrier, a dirty bandage over one eye and all across one ear. The closing dark was in their favour, but he was convinced the smell of his fear must be apparent to the waiting women around him. He positioned himself to the right so that his right ear and eye were unimpeded, and had to turn his head and squint to glimpse over to the left where Archie had placed himself next to an old woman who seemed to be alone, except for a baby strapped to her chest with a cloth. She had her *Kennkarte* in her hand. Thank God. It looked the same as Archie's. Archie caught Peter's eye briefly, then looked away.

When the train arrived it was the usual stampede. Peter thought his heart might burst out of his chest. He kept his head bowed, and held up his pass. *Please God,* he prayed wordlessly, his attention on the shuffling clogs of the woman in front, and her ragged hem.

A furtive glance sideways. The smooth-cheeked men at the barrier wore armbands and the caps with the eagle insignia. Appropriate enough, for their intent expressions reminded him of hawks scanning their prey.

Now. He pushed his way forward.

Nobody stopped him.

On the other side his head swam. He realised he hadn't been breathing. He sucked in great gasps of air. The train doors swayed open but the train was already inching forward. He turned desperately to look over his shoulder. Archie was behind him. He nearly yelled with euphoria. They'd done it.

He could not put all his weight on to his bad foot to lift himself up the carriage step, but was finally pushed up by the crush of people behind him, whilst those in front kept him upright.

There were not enough seats so they were standing. A German child in grubby lederhosen moved over to let Archie sit next to his mother. It brought a lump to his throat. So there was still politeness somewhere in this world. The train rattled off to the audible relief of those on board. Their progress would likely be slow. Peter recalled the awful train journey to Lamsdorf, and how they had to wait hours in sidings whilst other trains, presumably carrying German troops or supplies, passed them.

After a few hours nobody had been to collect their tickets so Peter relaxed a little. He made eye contact briefly with Archie and managed to find a squatting place near the door. At last he was able to get the weight off his leg which he stuck out in front of him, wedged in the doorway. The train jug-a-jugged into the darkness.

He must have slept because when he woke a station guard was standing over him asking him for a ticket. 'Dresden,' he said, holding out a *Reichsmark* note from Annegret's bag. The man wound the handle on his machine and the ticket issued. Peter nodded and took the ticket and change, went to put it in his pocket.

'*Frontsoldat?*' the guard asked.

Peter did not at first hear him, so he didn't reply. 'Shell shock,' said another passenger in German. 'I've seen it before.'

The guard moved off down the train shouting for everyone to put the blinds down now it was dark. Only then did Peter look to Archie. He was resting, his mouth hanging open, head back against the seat. And Peter slept once more. He was awoken by the sound of shelling. A deep rumble and boom of explosions. It suddenly occurred to him that the train could be strafed by Allied aircraft.

The lights in the train went out. Peter pulled up the blind to look out. He heard the drone of aircraft. Ahead of him he could see the distant wispy glow of target flares landing: Christmas trees, they called them. Children began to whimper. Unease manifested itself in the shifting of baggage. Others near the windows lifted the blinds hesitantly to peer out. The train creaked slowly, stop-starting. The faint thud of explosions. *Our boys,* Peter thought, *giving them what for.*

All seemed to be peaceful again. Peter looked out to see a distant orange glow on the horizon. For a moment the train picked up speed and then a deep boom shuddered up through the tracks and under their feet. The woman next to Archie gasped, and her little boy clambered squealing on to her knee.

More shelling followed, the echo first seeming close, then far away. He wondered what targets were being hit by these bombers. He could see no searchlights or other defences lighting up the sky, except for that weird orange glow on the horizon. The train picked up speed, though the sharp crack of explosions was louder. By now people were crowding to the windows to look under the blinds, eyes fixed on the horizon before them.

'Is that Dresden?' a young woman asked.

'No. Böhlen, maybe. Can't be Dresden. Must be the oil factory.'

But as they drew nearer, the glow in the distance became a roaring tower of flame. Now the noise of bombs had stopped. Grey smoke blanketed the sky. The train trundled nearer and nearer. Peter sought Archie's eyes. They met and held his before another small explosion caused Archie to lean over and stare, like everyone else, out of the window.

It seemed interminable, the long slow journey towards that orange glow. Now dark silhouettes were hurrying past them through the fields, and every road was clogged with the slow-moving shapes of cars and carts. In the distance, a lone siren wailed, but ahead, the whole horizon was ablaze and the black hulks of buildings were dwarfed by flames. The acrid smell of smoke seeped into the carriage. Several people coughed.

'*Gott in Himmel.*' The young woman next to Archie crossed herself.

The drone of more aircraft could be heard faintly over the noise of the train. People crowded to the windows to look out. Above them a cohort of planes flew in formation, so many they could be seen on both sides of the train, their dark fuselages visible against the grey smoke above. The compartment erupted into chaos. People screamed to get off. Peter stood up, swaying to find his balance, afraid he would be pushed out of the moving train.

The first hit was a crack followed by a deep roar. It rocked the train so it rattled on the rails. The ground shook. It was followed by more, wave after wave. In the compartment some women threw themselves to the ground. The carriage grew hot, the air dense. Surely the driver was not going to keep going? As they reached the suburbs a huge blast caused a clatter of debris to hit the train roof, and fiery fragments rained down either side of them. The train slowed, crawled onwards another four or five hundred yards. To their left another bomb fell. The train stuttered to a halt.

There was silence. Nobody wanted to get off now.

The train wheezed and creaked. Then slowly it inched backwards away from the station.

The woman next to Archie was weeping now, wringing a rosary in her hands.

The train shunted about a quarter of a mile back up the track and stopped. Outside a voice shouted, '*Raus!*'

The doors clanged open and smoke hit them like a wall.

They were to get off. Here. In the middle of nowhere.

There was a scramble to get baggage from the racks and to get out. Some were relieved, others terrified. Peter fell and rolled from the train; it was a long drop from the step. When he stood, he saw the old woman he'd followed onto the train; she was hesitating in the doorway, too frightened to jump, the baby clutched to her chest. Peter reached up his arms. She dithered a moment before handing the child over, then she too had to be helped down. Even in the darkness he was aware that the air was full of smuts, floating in front of his eyes. When he passed the baby back, its face was peppered with black ash.

He looked down the line and saw the doors disgorging their passengers. From inside the train, more shouting: '*Alle raus!*' Everyone off. Some people were already walking towards the blazing city. Others were arguing, some refusing to go.

Archie appeared by his side. 'Did you see those Lancasters?'

'Bloody frightening.'

'Do you think that's the end of it?'

'Don't know,' Peter said. 'But I hope Annegret and Klara are in a shelter somewhere.'

'They will be. She's tough. Dear God, it would be ironic if we got killed by our own bombers,' Archie whispered.

Peter pulled Archie to sit on the embankment. In the distance there was a roaring like the noise of wind through a tunnel. Another explosion briefly flared and a flurry of sparks showered upwards.

'You're not still thinking we should go there, are you?'

'Not until the morning. Give the fire crews some time to get to it. I want to see if Annegret and Klara are all right. And she'll want the photographs, I kept Dieter's picture, in my pocket. We can take her suitcase back to her.'

Peter didn't answer. They both knew that would be the last thing on Annegret's mind. But Archie was pretending they were in a world where a suitcase mattered. Peter said, 'Do you think that's what it looks like in London?'

Archie drew his breath in, shook his head. 'I don't know. Don't talk about it.'

***

Peter slept a while, huddled with Archie for warmth, arms round each other. It was a comfort to hear Archie's heart beating. In the morning he woke to find his throat hoarse, his eyes prickling with the effects of smoke.

Around him there were many more people, some from the train, some escapees from Dresden. The smell of burned cloth was everywhere. In daylight they saw that the fire was still raging. The sky was dense with soot. Not a single train had come out of Dresden the whole night.

'It looks pretty bad,' Archie said in a low voice. 'They haven't got the fire under control yet.'

'They'll be all right,' Peter replied.

Around midday the vibration of distant engines forced the refugees to look to the skies, hastily scramble their possessions together and take cover in ditches. They could not see the planes, but the whine of their engines went right over their heads.

'Not again,' Peter said, as another explosion made the horizon shake.

'Christ,' Archie cried, grabbing Peter and dragging him back down the embankment.

It was one of the longest forty-five minutes in his life. The explosions shuddered his heart in his chest; though he had his hands over his ears the noise was almost unbearable. He felt the blows might knock the earth off its axis. More hot, molten debris rained down on the train track. Archie clung to him as if he could keep him from falling apart.

When it was over, they lay still a very long time, just grateful to be alive.

Peter looked into Archie's eyes. They mirrored his own. Shock, disbelief. He turned away from him, staggered to his feet. Nobody could survive under such a blizzard of bombing. That this sort of thing happened, he knew, but he could not grasp that his own countrymen were responsible.

They watched the city burn for another day before they picked their way towards it through the charred countryside. They did not look to the sides; they dared not. Peter was aware only of Archie. As they neared the city they came across bodies of people who must have been running, their clothes and hair burned away.

Peter and Archie were the only people walking to Dresden; everyone else was limping away. Peter struggled with his stick, their progress slow. It did not seem to matter. He had lost track of which side he was supposed to be on, what the war was supposed to be for, what his orders were. After all these years, what he'd been fighting for seemed remote; he couldn't remember. He was simply following Archie. As they grew closer, what met their eyes was not a city. Not a single building had four walls; rubble smoked everywhere, as high as a man.

Somewhere underneath there lay the population of Dresden.

A charred bicycle lay on its side in the road with the remains of a man consumed by flames. Trams were half-buried under blackened masonry. A burned-out car lay before them surrounded by a tangled charred heap of bodies.

Archie baulked at walking past it. 'I don't think I can do this,' he said.

Peter stopped too in the road. He didn't want to look, but his eyes were drawn there anyway. 'We don't have to. We can go back.'

'I have to know if they're dead.' It was the first time Archie had admitted the possibility.

'It will be worse in the centre.'

Worse. The word had lost its meaning. They walked further. Each step a new horror. More bodies. The buildings still smouldering. The place was pleasantly warm, from the stones that had retained the heat. Peter began to sweat for the first time in years. It was eerily quiet. The bombed-out windows stared blankly as he and Archie manoeuvred their way over the pitted landscape.

Peter wiped his eyes. He was weeping, the sort of tears that just flowed mysteriously from somewhere, even though his mind was so numb with what he was seeing he could not even think. Or perhaps it was just the smoke.

A few people passed them, their red-rimmed eyes the only part of their face exposed, their clothes blackened. Everyone had their face covered with a scarf or cloth, and Archie and Peter soon did the same. They walked over molten solidified tar with debris that had been glued to the road. Peter saw shoes embedded in it, a pair of blackened high-heels. There was no sign of the woman who would have worn them. When they came to a crossroads a work party crossed right in front of them, grey-faced British prisoners of war armed with picks and shovels. Two dazed-looking armed guards followed behind.

A man dragging a small wheeled wooden cart full of unrecognisable charred items passed them, his head down. Peter couldn't be sure, but he thought it was a child's body.

Peter took hold of Archie's arm; he could bear it no longer. 'Let's go.' He was ashamed. They shouldn't be there; it was disrespectful. There had been rumours that the Germans had committed atrocities, but nothing could match this. 'Come on,' he said again, more urgently.

Another old woman was limping towards them. Archie shook Peter off and called after the woman. '*Bitte, wo ist die Engelstrasse?*'

She turned. '*Da. Kaputt. Alles, mein Leben, meine Kinder. Alles weg.*' She pointed up the road. It was the voice of a young woman, made old in one night. Peter understood her words: Gone. The whole city has gone. My whole life. My children. All gone.

Archie went a few steps forward before he stopped, his hands coming up to his head. He squatted down in the road as if to make himself as small as possible, like a foetus curled in on himself.

Ahead of him the centre of the city was a blackened hollow crater surrounded by the silhouettes of broken masonry.

Peter took Archie gently under the arm and guided him away from Dresden following the railway tracks, the way they had come. He was exhausted from limping so far with his stick and because the hope that had given them strength was gone.

'We should be dead,' Archie said, suddenly stopping. 'Why aren't we dead, Pete?'

'I don't know. Guess God has other plans.'

'God. You don't believe in him, do you?'

'No. Not now, no.' It was true. He didn't see that there could be any logic for a God. If he existed, why did he keep one person alive and not another? Why let Annegret and Klara escape death at the hands of the Red Army, make them walk all that way, then kill them in Dresden? *It isn't God, it's us*, he thought. *It's always been us.*

Archie sat on the embankment and took out of his pocket the pencil drawing that Klara had done on their way to Spremberg. He unfolded it on his knee. On it the house was still upright, all its windows and doors still there. The sun was shining its spiky little beams, and chickens still pecked lopsidedly by the wonky picket fence.

Without a word he folded it again and put it back in his pocket. A small tic moved at the corner of his mouth. Peter reached his hand out to put it on Archie's shoulder. As his hand made contact, Archie crumpled.

'What's the point?' he asked. 'What's the damn bloody point?'

There was no answer because Peter didn't really even know what he was asking him. Archie himself probably did not know what he was asking. The big questions are always the ones you can't even ask.

About Author Jean Gill:
Dave's niece and editor

I'm a Welsh writer and photographer living in the south of France with two scruffy dogs, a beehive named 'Endeavour', a Nikon D750 and a man. I taught English in Wales for many years and my claim to fame is that I was the first woman to be a secondary headteacher in Carmarthenshire. I'm mother or stepmother to five children so life has been pretty hectic.

I've published all kinds of books, both with traditional publishers and self-published. You'll find everything under my name from prize-winning poetry and novels, military history, translated books on dog training, to a cookery book on goat cheese. My work with top dog-trainer Michel Hasbrouck has taken me deep into the world of dogs with problems, and inspired one of my novels. With Scottish parents, an English birthplace and French residence, I can usually support the winning team on most sporting occasions.

www.jeangill.com

For news, offers and a FREE ebook of 'One Sixth of a Gill', please visit www.jeangill.com and sign up for my newsletter. This collection of shorts was a finalist in the Wishing Shelf and SpASpa Awards

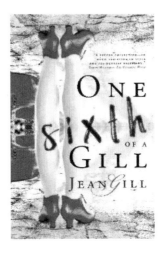

A book with 'Wow' factor - Geoff Nelder, *Aria*
A fantastic array of wonderful prose, from bee-keeping to Top Tips on Dogs! A FINALIST and highly recommended - The Wishing Shelf Awards

Five-minute reads. Meet people you will never forget: the night photographer, the gynaecologist's wife, the rescue dog. Dip into whatever suits your mood, from comedy to murders; from fantastic stories to blog posts, by way of love poetry.

Fully illustrated by the author; Jean Gill's original photographs are as thought-provoking as her writing. An out of body experience for adventurous readers. Or, of course, you can 'Live Safe'.

Not for you
the blind alley on a dark night,
wolf-lope pacing you step for step
as shadows flare on the walls.

29186324R00090

Printed in Great Britain
by Amazon